To Mum,
love from Traces xx

Traces X Christopher
August 2008

TAKING CHANCES

One Woman's Painful Journey to Self-Awareness and Survival

by

F.X. Christodoulou

AuthorHouse™ UK Ltd.
500 Avebury Boulevard
Central Milton Keynes, MK9 2BE
www.authorhouse.co.uk
Phone: 08001974150

This novel is entirely a work of fiction. The names, characters and incidents in it, apart from those already in the public domain, are the work of the author's imagination. Any resemblance to actual persons, living or dead is entirely coincidental.

© 2008 F.X. Christodoulou. All rights reserved.

No part of this book may be reproduced, stored in a retrieval system, or transmitted by any means without the written permission of the author.

First published by AuthorHouse 7/23/2008

ISBN: 978-1-4343-8157-6 (sc)

Printed in the United States of America
Bloomington, Indiana

This book is printed on acid-free paper.

For my children, Clare, Cheryl and Andrew

*And for my dear husband, Costas,
who encouraged me to write*

When any two young people take it into their heads to marry, they are pretty sure by perseverance to carry their point, be they ever so poor, or ever so imprudent, or ever so little likely to be necessary to each other's ultimate comfort.
Jane Austen, *Persuasion*

There is not one in a hundred of either sex, who is not taken in when they marry. Look where I will, I see that it *is so*; and I feel it *must* be so, when I consider that it is, of all transactions, the one in which people expect most from others, and are least honest themselves...........
Jane Austen, *Mansfield Park*

If she had been faultless, she would not have been the heroine of this story; for I think some wise man of old remarked, that the perfect women were those who left no histories behind them.
Mary Elizabeth Braddon, *Aurora Floyd*

All the changes and chances of this mortal life .....
The Book of Common Prayer

CHAPTER ONE

Plateau State, Nigeria: January 1980

It was another white hot day. Anna could feel the sweat trickling from her forehead and from under her arms, as she unlocked the car door and gingerly fingered the red hot steering wheel. It was only ten o'clock, but the heat already seemed to be palpable, rising from the ground as well as beating down from the clear blue and unrelenting sky.

Jos, the capital of Plateau State, where Anna and her family lived, was in truth, nothing like as hot as most parts of Nigeria. It had a fairly temperate climate, though it could still be very hot in the day; however, it was a dry heat, and the nights were cool, so it was a lot more comfortable for sleeping than the more hot and humid areas of the country. It was located high on the Jos Plateau and had been important as a centre for tin mining during the period of British colonial rule. The town was then known as a hill station, and was popular as a holiday destination for the British colonial administrators, when they had local leave, just as their counterparts in India frequented hill stations such as Simla and Pankot.

Jos was still a sought after placement for expatriates and Nigerians alike, in the present day, and it was also seen as an attractive holiday destination for tourists, expatriates and Nigerians from other parts of the country. The most prestigious hotel in Jos was named The Hill Station Hotel, in recognition of its historical status and desirable location. Anna went there sometimes for a meal or drinks with family and friends, if they felt like a special treat. It was situated at the top of a hill, had a substantial white multi-storey exterior, and was set in attractive gardens, surrounded by palm trees and other exotic plants. Inside it felt pleasantly cool in the air conditioned lounges, and in the restaurant, with its starched white table napkins and attentive uniformed waiters; the service was excellent, almost a remnant from colonial days, and it always felt like a luxurious and extravagant outing.

Today was Saturday, still quite early in the morning, and Anna and her husband were giving a party for friends and colleagues from the university that evening. Anna had finally been able to extricate herself from her three children who had been left, at first protesting, and then requesting various goodies from the shops, with their baby nurse, a seventeen year old local village girl. Anna never felt really relaxed about leaving the children with the girl, always fearing that Dorcas might be negligent or impatient with them, but too often there was no real alternative.

When she went to work, even though the two eldest children went to school, she had to leave her baby boy in Dorcas's care, and always felt sick with fear that something might go wrong. She remembered the horror story she had heard about a baby nurse who had put the baby, rather than the feeding bottle, in the fridge, as she had been instructed. So far all had been well, apart from the girls reporting that Dorcas, in her zeal to feed the baby, had once removed the teat from his bottle, and had attempted to pour the milk directly into Femi's mouth, despite protests from his sisters.

Today Anna needed to get the shopping done quickly, and could not afford the time required to prepare the children for the outing, and then to try to move round the store for her necessities, with them in tow. If they had come along there would be the inevitable delays to accommodate requests for goodies, toys and detours to look at favourite departments.

As she drove through the university housing complex, Anna saw, without really registering, the familiar bungalows in their large compounds, many of the yards containing pretty trees and shrubs, their green leaves contrasting with the arid brown earth around them. In some there were children playing under the trees or in the dusty yards; in others servants were hanging out washing, chatting and laughing, whilst engaged in carrying out various household tasks, like pounding yam or preparing vegetables. So many activities in Nigeria were carried out in the open air, instead of behind closed doors, as they had to be in the cold northern European countries. Nigeria, being located in West Africa, was very close to the equator and so had a tropical climate. Even during the rainy season, as soon as a heavy rain storm had vanished, the sun would shine down with its usual intensity, causing the wet ground to dry and heat up again very rapidly, steam rising from it, like a white mist, for the first few minutes after the rain ceased.

As she drove, Anna counted her blessings. She had an interesting and quite easy job, teaching English at the university, a comfortable university bungalow with servants to take care of the chores, and a handsome and successful husband. Indeed her husband was eyed hungrily by both the bored expatriate wives, who lay around the swimming pools all day long in their skimpy bikinis, on the lookout for fit male bodies, black or white; and voluptuous expensively clad female students, flaunting their fashions and their availability on the campus. The former hoped for some diversion on the side, and the latter were always on the alert for chances of identifying a promising 'sugar daddy'. Rumours about relationships between students and lecturers abounded, with hints of sexual blackmail demanded by these lecturers – either you sleep with me or you will fail your exams. Most of the students were not in a position to refuse, and many capitalised on their charms in order to acquire other favours. Anna trusted Shola almost completely, as he duly reported all or most of the advances made to him by different women. However it could be unsettling to be reminded how much some of them coveted what she had.

Soon she turned out of the university complex and immediately had to concentrate more carefully on her driving. Now, instead of the near deserted campus roads, she had to drive through dusty narrow streets lined with little shops and houses and roadside stalls; street hawkers of all ages and genders, wearing a variety of colourful African and European garb, with large trays on their heads, were weaving their way through people and animals; chickens squawked, while small piglets and large goats competed for space with harassed shoppers. Ditches full of putrid effluent, used for waste disposal and often for toilet purposes, lined the narrow streets, which made them even more difficult to negotiate, both by car, and most crucially on foot. Parked vehicles left at every conceivable angle, and people haggling over prices, added to the general cacophony and chaos, and motorists drove with hands firmly on their car horns to force their way through.

By force of habit and sheer persistence, Anna finally arrived at her destination – the one and only department store in Jos - Kingsway, patronised by affluent Nigerians and expatriates alike. The modern air conditioned three storey building towered above the smaller and simpler shops around it. On days when consignments of items like Irish butter arrived, shoppers descended on the store like locusts; the expatriates, and locals alike, were to be seen with loaded trolleys full of limited imported luxuries, even though the store stipulated a strict limit per family on such goods.

Having found a place to park, Anna had then to run the gauntlet of the outstretched hands of the crowd of beggars, who surrounded the entrance of the store. Some of the beggars, 'burnt out' leprosy cases, held out mutilated claws with missing fingers like creatures from a horror movie; others dragged themselves on the ground in an undignified shuffle. Here disadvantage and deformity appeared so stark compared to the UK, where hideous afflictions are hidden behind closed doors or confined to wheel chairs. How welcome a wheelchair would be for some of these unfortunates! Anna always felt a sense of guilt on seeing these pathetic human beings, and usually thrust a coin into one or two outstretched limbs on her way out of the building. She hated herself for the disgust she felt, and her failure to look these people fully in the eyes.

Today as she scurried into the store she hardly noticed the beggars milling around the entrance. She headed for the household section to purchase some last minute items: paper napkins, plates and cups; some cocktail sticks, and a few artificial flowers to put on the table. The party would be a simple affair: just some jollof rice and chicken, plates of stuffed eggs and other buffet style foods, and of course, plenty of cold beer and other alcoholic and soft drinks. The drinks had been bought the previous day as had most of the other foodstuffs. Mindful of the children at home, she also picked up a few bars of the much coveted and highly prized Cadbury's chocolate, as the store seemed to have acquired a new stock.

Now as she stood impatiently, in a long queue at the checkout, Anna became conscious of a young European woman, probably about her own age, standing in front of her, a little mixed race child clutched to her chest. The woman appeared slightly dishevelled. However, she presented a very striking appearance, with her tall willowy figure, and her long red hair caught up in a loose bun. She was wearing a colourful Nigerian outfit made of blue and green tie-dyed cotton material, comprising a loose blouse and full length skirt. Anna suddenly recalled seeing a similar woman, conspicuous particularly because of the colour of her hair, standing waiting for the student bus, the only European amongst a crowd of young Nigerian students. She remembered now that she had felt a passing interest in the identity of the woman, and had then forgotten about her until this moment. She smiled and the woman smiled back, though she seemed preoccupied with her own thoughts.

'You have a lovely little boy', Anna remarked as they waited.

'Thanks. His name is Dipo. He's my youngest. I have a girl at home. She's five. Have we met before?'

'I'm not sure. Not formally at least. I think I've seen you on the campus.'

'Well, that's certainly a possibility. I'm as student. I'm studying for a B.Ed. I've been sponsored by a girls' grammar school. It's a hard slog, but at least it will mean I will be independent. My name's Dorothy Adekunle.'

'I'm Anna Banjo'. I'm a lecturer at the uni. I hope we run into one another again soon. I've got to dash now as we're having a party tonight. Would you be able to come?'

'I'd love to, but I don't think I can make it tonight. Thanks for asking. Have you got an office on the campus?'

'Yes, it's in B Block – number 103. Do pop in sometime and we can have a chat.'

'Thanks. That would be lovely. I hope your party goes well.'

'I hope so too. It's been really nice to meet you. I'd better be off now as the kids will be getting anxious. Bye.'

Anna watched Dorothy and Dipo disappear into the crowded street and then she made for her car. 'I wish we weren't having this party tonight,' she thought. 'Still, Shola likes to make an impression on his friends so I'll have to do my best.'

Anna was a woman who always wanted to please everyone, and often ended up pleasing no one, especially not herself. She was also a rather timid person, anxious to avoid confrontation or arguments, usually taking the line of least resistance, unless her back was really against the wall. Then she would strike out in self defence, occasionally going overboard in her reaction. When it was a choice between either 'fight or flight,' the latter was her invariable strategy. In order to get what she wanted, she tended, albeit unconsciously, to have a passive aggressive approach, using subtle persuasion rather than demands, and developing a secretive, and sometimes manipulative, response to problems and difficulties.

This trait in her character was exacerbated because of the kind of man she was married to. Although she loved him dearly, she would be the first to admit that Shola was a domineering man, who expected compliance from her, and was unwilling to compromise in any argument. He could, however, sometimes be nudged into changing his stance, as long as he felt he had decided this himself, and had not been forced into anything.

On the way back, Anna could not help wondering about Dorothy and whether she ever felt the way that she did herself. Despite her privileged life, Anna often felt homesick, not so much for people left behind in England, but for the feel of the country: the cool dampness compared to this perpetual heat and dust; the sense of order, security and predictability of life there, at least in her nostalgic imagination, and also a sense of belonging. Now she imagined she knew how black people must feel in the UK – always the object of scrutiny and disapproval, being immediately visible as different and alien. That's what I am here, she thought. I always stand out as a foreigner, with my pale anaemic looks, contrasting unfavourably with the healthy black faces around me. Whether I am called an *oyingbo* in Yoruba, or a *bature* in Hausa, it is always a kind of pejorative label based on my racial appearance. I can never be just another anonymous person, like everyone else.

Then she hastily corrected herself about her own interpretation of these labels as being negative; possibly this was how she viewed herself, wistfully wishing that she too was black. Her train of thought took her back a few years to an incident, trivial in itself, that had left an indelible impression on her. It had happened a few months after her first arrival in Nigeria, and at the time they had been living in Ibadan, a large and sprawling city in the south west of the country. A young English woman acquaintance, Linda Smith, who was married to a fellow Brit, had invited Anna to accompany her and her baby daughter, who must have been about ten months old at the time, to a very large market in the city. This was to be Anna's first trip to a Nigerian market, and she was intrigued, but not a little apprehensive about it, unsure of what awaited her.

Linda was driving a sturdy black station wagon, and her baby, a very blonde, blue eyed little girl, was strapped in her baby chair on the back seat of the car. When they reached the perimeter of the market and parked, Anna was fascinated to observe the milling crowds of shoppers and traders, most of whom were dressed in colourful traditional Yoruba attire, hot under the merciless sun, busy selecting and haggling over goods, whether meat, vegetables, locally woven cloth or silver and gold jewellery. Most of the traders had their own stalls, but hawkers of oranges, boiled eggs, nuts and other produce, carried in large trays balanced on their heads, mingled with shoppers, hoping for hungry or thirsty housewives or servants to be tempted to buy from them.

'Anna, would you mind if I left Suzy with you in the car, while I go to buy some meat. It's so difficult to carry her through all the crowds, and I won't be more than a few minutes?' Linda asked.

'That's fine,' responded Anna, secretly hoping that Linda would not leave them too long. She was unused to babies, and had no idea what to do if Suzy started crying.

When Linda had disappeared into the crowd, Anna eyed Suzy dubiously, but smiled at the baby, and talked to her in the way she had heard others talk to babies. After a few minutes she became aware that the baby's eyes were fixed on something outside the car; Anna herself had been so busy looking at Suzy that she had been completely oblivious to anything else. When she followed the baby's gaze, she was astonished to see that the car was now completely surrounded by people, many of them children, all pointing at Suzy and shouting, '*Oyingbo, oyingbo.*' Suzy's little face puckered up, and she began screaming at the top of her tiny voice, growing scarlet in the process. Anna did not know whether to be more concerned about Suzy, or the crowds outside the car. If only Linda would come back! The crowd seemed to have increased, and Anna could only see a mass of black faces, noses pressed against the window panes of the car, and she could feel herself growing even hotter than she had been already, and having no idea what to do. Suzy's screams grew louder, and Anna tried vainly to comfort her. Where on earth was Linda?

After what seemed hours, but was probably about fifteen minutes, Linda reappeared clutching her shopping, and with a wave to the assembled crowd, nonchalantly opened the door of the car, and climbed into the driving seat. As soon as Suzy saw her mother, she stopped crying. The crowd dispersed, and they drove off, Anna feeling very foolish for being so scared, and so ineffectual.

When she thought about it afterwards, Anna realised that the crowd, far from being hostile, were just fascinated to see the blonde baby, possibly the first one they had ever seen so close to them. They were admiring her, and their shouts were of praise and wonder, not disdain or dislike. This was, of course, how most of the Nigerians she came across, particularly the common people in the streets or markets, perceived white people, not with hatred or negativity, but with interest and admiration. Very different indeed to how Nigerians were perceived in Britain by most white people on the street. In truth, the only hostility Anna had received in Nigeria was occasionally from Nigerians, who had studied abroad, and who had been subjected to racism themselves, and now felt like getting their own back. Anna did not blame them.

She returned to her earlier musing. What do I really mean by 'belonging'? she asked herself, as she negotiated the narrow streets on her drive home. Maybe it's just a desire not to always be conspicuously different and other. I'd love to be able to merge into the crowd without people noticing me, or trying to attract my attention, or getting me to buy something in the market at an inflated price. Well, maybe it won't go on like this for ever. I'll just have to see how long I can stand it. I owe it to Shola to try and make a go of our life as a family in this country. After all, we've been through such a lot together already, to get to where we are today.

Feeling very ashamed of her negative feelings, she remonstrated with herself firmly, I really must pull myself together. There's no point in daydreaming, or fighting my situation in the here and now. I have so much to be grateful for, my husband, my children, my home and my job, so I should be more positive. Anyway, I haven't got time to think about this now. I'd better concentrate on getting back in good time, and helping to prepare for this party, or everyone will be wondering where on earth I've got to.

CHAPTER TWO

By the time that Anna turned into her lane, she could already hear the sound of booming soul music coming from her bungalow. The open windows and doors allowed the music to drift out into the surrounding neighbourhood; it was just as well that Nigerians did not have a problem with noise. How different from England, where such a racket would mean that the police might be called, especially if the people having the party were black. The fact that the music was already being played meant that Shola was busy arranging the lounge for the party.

Shola loved loud music, particularly when he was occupied with some physical task. Unlike many men, Shola enjoyed ironing and would spend hours pressing his shirts and suits, and often Anna managed to include some of her own and the children's clothes for his expert attention. While he ironed, Shola would listen to an eclectic mix of his favourite vinyl including soul, jazz, country and western, Bing Crosby, James Brown, Stevie Wonder and reggae. Now as he arranged tables and chairs, checked that there were enough drinks in the fridge and ordered the houseboys, Joseph and Mustafa, to clean more thoroughly and re-arrange the furniture, he appeared excited and happy. As usual he had a cigarette in his mouth, which he removed to greet Anna.

Her husband, Shola, was in some ways a larger than life character. He was tall, over six feet in height, and of slender build. His complexion was medium brown in colour, and he had well defined mobile features, an imposingly high forehead and expressive dark brown eyes. He had a mercurial temperament, and his expression could change from good humoured to angry in seconds. Despite this, his charismatic character attracted attention, and he was considered very handsome, and extremely good company, by men and women alike. When he was happy, as he was now, he radiated a vibrant energy, which was infectious; when he was annoyed, his eyes would flash, and his negative energy would permeate the environment. He had a deep attractive voice, which could however, turn menacing and frightening if anything upset him.

'Did you manage to get those things?' he asked, smiling at Anna. 'I think everything is under control here, but you still need to get the eggs finished and also check on the preparation of the chicken and rice.'

'Yes, I think I've got all the things on my list. Are the kids ok?'

'As far as I know, they're fine. They're in their room with Dorcas.'

'Right, I'll go and check on them before I start in the kitchen. By the way, do you remember that white woman I said I had seen waiting for the student bus about a month ago? Well, I saw her today at Kingsway and we had a little chat.'

'Oh, you mean Mrs Adekunle.'

'How do you know her name? I only found it out today'.

'I asked a couple of people and I heard that she is married to a rather hopeless chap – he is the manager of one of the small guesthouses in town. Apparently he plays around a lot with the various women that frequent the place. It's no more than a glorified brothel. She must be really wretched.'

'Well, she did look rather sad. Anyway, I gave her my office number and invited her to drop in sometime.'

'Ok, but I'm warning you – don't get involved.'

※

Anna forgot about Dorothy for the next few hours, as she busied herself with tending to the children's needs and preparing for the party. When everything was ready, she got changed into a fairly new black dress with frills around the neckline, and surveyed herself in the mirror. Anna had never been vain; on the contrary she had always considered herself quite ordinary. However, tonight she felt pleased with her appearance. Her short dark curly hair had been recently cut and set, her figure looked almost svelte in the dress, and her black patent leather high-heels showed her legs to advantage.

'Mummy, you look lovely,' was the consensus from the children when she went to say goodnight.

※

The party was the usual thing: various couples, a mix of African, African-American, white-American, British and other assorted Europeans. Some of the couples were both Nigerian, others mixed, but all were out to enjoy themselves as much as possible at someone else's expense. A few of the guests were good friends of Shola and Anna, but many were mere acquaintances, mostly colleagues from the university or other professionals from the town. Drinks flowed like water (possibly more freely considering that the water supply was very unpredictable); plates were emptied and refilled; soon couples were dancing and everyone seemed happy. Anna herself loved to dance with her tall handsome husband, and let herself relax, responding to the beat of the music. Aware of his arms around her, and the envious looks of some of the other women, the time flew by almost unnoticed.

Later in the evening an argument broke out when one of the Nigerians made a play for the Russian wife of another. Shola, always good in these situations managed to calm things down, and eventually the culprit subsided in a corner, passing out in an alcoholic stupor. When the time came for the party to break up, this man could not be woken, despite numerous attempts at calling his name and even shaking him. His poor wife, an uneducated, rather mousy British girl from Manchester, was in a pitiable state, and she had two of her older girls with her. Once again, Shola dealt with this delicate predicament. With the help of another guest he managed to half carry and half drag Yemi to a car, bundling him in unceremoniously. Then he drove the family to the hotel where they were staying for the weekend, as they actually lived in another state.

※

While Shola was away, Anna started to do some half-hearted clearing up, having changed out of her party dress into her nightdress and dressing gown. It was now the small hours of the morning and she felt exhausted. As she worked she thought about Shola and how they had first met. Both had been students at Manchester University in the late sixties, and had been immediately attracted to each other when they met at a departmental party. Shola was studying for a Ph.D in English, while Anna was an undergraduate. He had seemed so exciting and different to the rather spotty and pasty-faced boys that Anna had dated previously. He was the archetypal tall, dark and handsome man, of course rather darker than the Jane Austen or Georgette Heyer model, but equally challenging and dangerous.

They both shared a passion for English literature and would discuss poetry and novels for hours. They went to the theatre,

Taking Chances

the cinema, dancing, and for long walks. They used to talk earnestly about their hopes for the future, and how they would defy the world in order to be together. They had encountered some hostility on the streets of Manchester, such as evil looks and some verbal abuse, and a few Polish landlords, who did not like black people as tenants, but they were undeterred by any kind of negativity.

They had dated for several months before she summoned up the courage to tell her parents that she was involved with an African. Some instinct had warned her that her parents would not be over the moon with her choice, especially as she was an only child, but nothing had prepared her for their actual reaction.

'Are you mad?' her father had expostulated. 'After all we have done for you!'

'You will kill your father,' had been her mother's comment, adding 'You know he has a heart condition.'

'I would have done anything for you, if you had chosen a man of your own race', her father had almost spat at her. 'But now you have disgraced us.'

Friends had comforted Anna, and assured her that her parents would come round eventually if she showed them that she would not be dissuaded. The friends were right to some extent; at least her parents did eventually agree to meet Shola and despite themselves were quite impressed with his knowledge and charm. They were never really happy about the relationship, coming from a lower middle –class area of Derbyshire, and had a narrow minded circle of friends. Her father worked for an insurance firm and her mother had always been a housewife. Anna's father was tall and quite distinguished in appearance, handsome in a very English way, with his silver hair and slightly florid complexion; her mother was a timid, rather non-descript woman, who worshipped her domineering husband and did not have any opinions of her own, or so it seemed to Anna. The more her parents opposed the match, the more Anna clung to

Shola. It was her life, not theirs. What did they know about the modern world?

Anna's mother wept silently throughout the wedding ceremony, as if she were at a funeral and not a marriage. Anna was not sure if her father would be 'giving her away' until the last minute. She had an uncle lined up as a substitute, in case his disapproval would preclude his participation in the ceremony. In the event he carried out his role, but in a joyless and resigned manner. In later years, both her parents embraced their grandchildren, but with always a slight reservation and martyred expressions - 'a pity about their hair' was a typical comment.

Anna's mother was now a widow, who never failed to remind Anna that her marriage had contributed to her father's ill-health, and by implication, death. Anna kept in touch with her mother by the occasional letter, but always had the impression that she preferred that Anna be 'abroad' and therefore not an embarrassment to her.

Shola's parents had not been impressed either.

'Why are you marrying a white woman? She will leave you. There are plenty of nice Yoruba girls to marry,' were some of their complaints.

Once again, they had come round eventually and they genuinely loved their grandchildren and were very proud of them. Shola's father, a truly kind and gentle man, always had a gift of pennies or sweets when they visited the little house in one of the suburbs of Lagos, and loved to take the children on his knee and make a fuss of them. His mother, a formidable lady, obviously once a great beauty, of whom Anna was more than a little afraid, also loved the children and was constantly urging Anna to add to their number. Tragically, both his parents had died within a very short period of time of each other, about three years previously, from long-standing illnesses. Medical services had been inadequate, and that combined with ignorance about their conditions, meant that they had succumbed to death comparatively young, both being only in their late middle age.

Shola had been traumatised and Anna always felt that these deaths had come between them; although Shola had not been particularly close to his parents, he now felt guilty that they had not spent more time with them, and Anna sensed that he consciously or unconsciously blamed her. Anna did in fact feel guilty about this and often made allowances for Shola's moods in recognition of his feelings.

※

After about an hour Anna heard Shola returning.
'How did it go?'
'Terrible. Yemi's wife and the girls made a run for it, when I stopped the car, and locked themselves in their hotel chalet. I left Yemi outside, hammering on the door and shouting abuse. I feel sorry for that family.'
'I agree. Poor Maureen! What a life! It makes me grateful for what we have.'
'That man is an oaf. He'll come to a bad end if he doesn't change his ways. Anyway, let's go to bed now. We can sort all this out in the morning when the houseboys are in.'
'Good idea. I'm proud of how you managed that situation, even though there was no way it could end well.'
Anna hugged Shola, and their arms and hands entwined, they walked towards the bedroom, both exhausted but united and content. Despite the one or two problems of the evening, their party had been a success and their guests had enjoyed a good time. Shola's status as a generous and charismatic host had been confirmed, and Anna was happy that she had been able to do her own part in assisting him to achieve the desired outcome. They were perceived as one of the most sociable couples at the university, big fish in a small pool, and that was exactly how Shola liked it.

CHAPTER THREE

The next day being Sunday they had a lie-in, and after breakfast prepared for their regular weekly visit to the staff club. The children were dressed in their Sunday best. The two girls were only two years apart in age, and Anna often dressed them alike. Today they were wearing matching dresses, made by a local seamstress in some striking African red and black design, printed on locally woven cotton material. Some rather short-sighted and unperceptive people often took the girls for twins, although they were not particularly similar in appearance and were obviously different in height. The elder daughter, Shade, was about ten, while her sister, Lola, was nearly eight; they were both extremely pretty little girls, with their black curly hair, dark eyes and coffee coloured skin.

Shade was very emotionally attached to Anna. She was a responsible and serious girl, who loved reading and cooking, and who also acted as a little mother to Femi when Anna busy.

Lola was a carefree child, her father's favourite, and she liked to follow him around when he was out in the yard attending to his bird-house, where he kept chickens, turkeys, ducks and even an African grey parrot.

Shola had designed the bird-house himself, and had supervised its building out of wood, corrugated iron and wire mesh, to ensure it was just as he wanted it. When he released the domestic birds from the bird-house each morning, the turkeys would strut around the compound, the male, with an attendant group of females, displaying his splendid tail feathers; scrawny hens would scratch in the dust, and cluck in protest as they were pursued by the colourful cockerels; and the ducks would waddle and quack, as they led their ducklings to the pool that Shola had provided for them.

Today, at the university staff club it was the usual routine. The club itself was designed so that members could sit inside or out by the pool. Inside there were a bar, tables and chairs and a billiards table, while outside, a swimming pool, filled with tempting blue water, reflecting the rays of the brilliant sun, was fringed with drooping palm trees, under which were placed loungers and small tables for drinks. Several of the expatriate staff could be seen, lying stretched out beside the pool, the women working on their tans, while displaying their bikini-clad bodies to maximum advantage. In their pursuit of the perfect skin tone, they eschewed both the shade of the palm trees, or the shelter of the covered bar. The inside area of the club was open on one side facing the pool, so that people could wander in and out freely.

Anna and Shola chose to sit inside, out of the sun, with a group of their friends. The adults sat around gossiping and drinking Star beer or soft drinks, while the children played about with each other, or children of friends. Anna kept a close eye on them, always fearing that they were going to knock over a small table covered in bottles and glasses, or get into some other kind of trouble. She was also wary of them running outside and falling into the pool, so she had to be constantly vigilant, while trying to join in the conversation with the others. As Femi was still an infant, he lay cooing in his baby chair beside her. He was a jolly, contented baby, with similar colouring to his two sisters, and was much praised and made a fuss of by everyone.

Unexpectedly, Shola raised the subject of Dorothy Adekunle, and several of their friends seemed to know of her. The general consensus was that she was a very unfortunate woman and they pitied her.

'Why on earth does she stay with that terrible man?' was the general female view, while predictably, most of the men seemed to think it was no one else's business. They did, however, all agree that her husband was a very stupid man.

※

On Monday, Anna went to work as usual. She had a nine o'clock lecture, but afterwards she would be free to work in her office until two, and the next teaching slot. After her lecture, Anna got herself a coffee, and then sat down at her desk to do some marking and plan her lectures for the following day.

Her office was on the first floor of the Humanities Building, and she was fortunate enough to have it to herself. It was a simple room, containing her desk, cluttered with books and files, facing the door, with her own work chair behind it; opposite her was placed another wooden chair, often occupied by students consulting her about their work. There was also a bookcase, full of reference books, and five wooden easy chairs with bright blue cushions, which she could use for her students when she had tutorials. A coffee table, placed in the central area surrounded by the five easy chairs, enhanced the comfortable, almost homely, feel to the room. An air conditioner wheezed and dripped in one corner, its noise effectively shutting out any sounds coming from the corridor or the yard below her window.

Anna was soon engrossed in what she was doing, and was shocked to look at her watch and discover that it was nearly

Taking Chances

lunchtime. As she was about to pack up, there was a gentle tap on her door.

'Come in.'

Anna looked up to see Dorothy, her new friend, nervously putting her head round the door.

'I hope I'm not disturbing you. I can come back another time.'

'No, it's fine. I was just about to pack up for lunch. Would you like to join me?'

'Will it be ok? After all, I'm just a student. I probably won't be welcome in the staff common room.'

'Don't worry. I'll go and get some sandwiches and soft drinks. We can eat here.'

'That will be great. Thanks so much.'

In fact, Anna rarely ate in the common room herself. She was not very popular with some of the expatriate staff, especially a few of the older Brits, as they considered her something of a traitor to her race. This situation had been brought about shortly after Anna started work at the university. She had been sitting in the common room, eating her sandwiches and drinking a cup of coffee, when she became aware of a conversation taking place near her, which she could not but overhear. When she looked around the room, she noticed that the only people present were white expatriates, the majority being British, and as such they were talking freely among themselves, assuming that she was 'one of them'.

Led by a particularly red faced and loud elderly lecturer, the group were discussing one of the older Nigerian professors in very disparaging terms, with obvious racial undertones. They referred to him as a 'silly old fool,' and added other unflattering epithets, which they would never have applied to a white man in a similar context. Anna was appalled, embarrassed, but said nothing and escaped from the room as soon as she was able to.

When she had got home, she had mentioned the incident to Shola, who outraged, had promptly reported it to the professor in question, which triggered some unpleasant repercussions. Needless to say, the Brits soon worked out who the informer was, especially when they learned that she was married to a Nigerian. From that day on, Anna never sat in the common room, preferring a solitary lunch in her own office, to running the risk of encountering a group of racists; racists who were happy enough to take academic jobs in Nigeria, at higher grades than they would have got in Britain, if they had been able to get jobs at all, to siphon money from Nigeria into their own bank accounts, and then abuse their employers into the bargain.

Anna ran down to the common room, purchased their lunch, and returned to her office to find Dorothy with her eyes closed, looking absolutely drained and exhausted.

Over lunch, Dorothy confirmed some of the rumours that Anna had heard.

'I'm trying to get a degree so that I can be independent of Jide. I would leave him and take the children back to England, but Jide won't hear of it. He agrees that he no longer loves me and he says I can leave if I want to, but he insists that he will keep the children. You understand that, as a mother, I couldn't leave my children behind. I think he knows this too, so he has got me where he wants me. I will have to stay here, get a teaching job and then possibly get my own place. I think he will allow me to have the children living with me, as long as we don't leave the country. He has warned me that he has relatives working at the international airports, who will stop me if I try to take the children back to the UK.'

'I'm really sorry to hear about your predicament,' Anna replied sympathetically. 'I only wish I could give you some positive advice, but I can't think of anything to say at this moment. But if there's any way you think I can help, please let me know. At least we can be friends and you will know that you have someone to confide in.'

Anna felt that her response and offers were totally inadequate, but could not think of anything else she could do at that time. She herself was constrained by what Shola would allow, in terms of getting involved in Dorothy's plight, and she would have to think of ways around this. All this made her feel uneasy too. What if she was in Dorothy's position? What would and could she do? A little trickle of fear, that shivery feeling that people say is 'someone is walking over your grave', went through her, which she immediately forced herself to suppress.

'Look, I have to get ready for my lecture now,' she said with a warm, and she hoped, comforting smile. 'Do pop in anytime you want to talk. And don't forget I'll be here for you and will try to help as much as I can.'

'Thanks so much. I do feel better for talking to you. I'll let you get on with your work now. I've got to get to a class myself.'

Dorothy left the office and shortly afterwards Anna went to give her afternoon lecture.

Dorothy's situation preyed on Anna's mind all day. She remembered an African-American friend she had known when she and Shola had been working at the University of Lagos, some years earlier, and how she had been in a similar position to Dorothy's. She had eventually managed to smuggle herself and her baby son out of the country and then to the US. She had later written to Anna from the States, very relieved and happy that she had made the decision to leave her unhappy marriage. If she had the courage, perhaps Dorothy could do the same, should it become necessary, although it would be much more difficult with two children.

❋

When Anna got home after picking up the girls from school, she was met by the baby nurse who seemed distressed and anxious.

'Madame, Femi sick. He very hot and no eat', she gasped, obviously near to tears.

Fear clutched Anna. She felt cold despite the heat. She rushed to the baby and picked him up. Yes, he was burning with fever. After leaving the girls, confused and upset, with the distraught Dorcas, she bundled her baby into the car and drove fast, even recklessly, to the university clinic. The clinic was a very basic one storey building, containing a waiting room, some treatment rooms, and of course, a couple of doctors' consulting rooms. There were other patients waiting there before them; it seemed hours to Anna before Femi was seen by a doctor. He lay weakly in her arms, his breathing so shallow that she could scarcely see or hear it, and it seemed to her that he could so easily slip away. She felt sick and weak with fear. She remembered now, as terrifying scenarios raced through her mind, that some colleagues at the university, the wife an African-American and her husband an Igbo, had lost a baby in similar circumstances.

'Please God, don't let him die,' Anna breathed.

The doctor prescribed anti-malarial injections and antibiotics. Apparently Femi had a urinary infection, but in Nigeria, almost all fevers were accompanied by malaria. Femi was injected by a buxom, very matter-of-fact nurse, who advised Anna to sponge her baby with cool water to bring down the fever, and to bring him back to the clinic for daily injections for the next week.

Anna carried the hot bundle back to the car and drove home. She sponged the little body repeatedly and gradually his temperature went down. Over, the next few days Anna devoted all her time to her son. Miraculously, or so it seemed to her, he recovered, growing stronger day by day, as the drugs did their work.

Exhausted by anxiety and terror, Anna started to wonder whether she could or should stay in this country, where babies could die so easily. This time she had been lucky, but would her luck hold out? What about the girls? Something terrible could happen to one of them. Would she survive if one of the children were lost? Suddenly, she felt afraid, and a wave of panic washed over her. Had she made a terrible mistake to settle here? Would Shola understand how she felt? Something was changing in her, but she didn't yet know where these disturbing feelings would lead.

CHAPTER FOUR

Anna had no time to brood on her fears for the next couple of weeks, as it was coming up to Christmas. She had never really become used to celebrating the festive season in the tropics. Christmas in her mind was still associated with wrapping up in thick coats, scarves and woolly hats, and donning heavy boots to trudge through wind and rain, if not snow, to do her Christmas shopping.

Here it felt like high summer all the year round, but nevertheless she tried to capture the spirit of the season, and attempt to replicate the Christmases of her childhood for her own children, times which she remembered with a fond nostalgia for some of the innocent pleasures of the past.

Anna rummaged in her store cupboards, and produced her stock of decorations. She pulled out glittering tinsel of different colours, shiny silver and gold baubles to hang on the tree, and finally the tree itself, an artificial green fir tree which looked quite realistic; she had been lucky enough to snap it up in Kingsway a couple of years previously. She soon realised that she needed to replenish the streamers, as some of them were looking dilapidated and bedraggled from use over the past few years, and she also felt that the tree could do with some additional decorations, including new fairy lights. She now remembered that their old ones had fused last New Year's Day, and they had not bothered to purchase any more. She would have to make a trip to Kingsway for these items, and of course, presents for the children and Shola, as well as other Christmas goodies, before they were all sold out.

It was the last day of the university term, and when she had given her morning lecture, Anna would be free for the rest of the day. She decided to drive directly to Kingsway from work, and she would have plenty of time for shopping before the girls finished school. She was due to attend a Carol Concert at the school the following afternoon, and she wanted to have most of her Christmas shopping done before this, because the school broke up after the concert and then she would have all the children to attend to for the duration of the holiday.

Kingsway was brightly decorated for Christmas. They even had a Santa Claus, who distributed gifts to the children for a small fee; Anna decided that she would bring her children before Christmas, as they would all enjoy seeing Father Christmas. She now had to get down to the serious business of her shopping. Whenever imported stock arrived in the store, especially at this time of the year, customers would perform their usual locust like descent, and if one was not quick off the mark, all the items would disappear in a matter of a few hours. It seemed that there was a form of 'bush telegraph', so that fortunate shoppers contacted their friends to inform them of the arrival of new stock.

Anna had been in the store the previous week, and a friendly assistant had informed her that they were expecting a consignment of books and other luxury items shortly. She hoped that they would have arrived by now, and that she would be one of the first to make her selection. Accordingly, she hastened to the book section, and to her delight she discovered that a large stock of children's books had just been unpacked and were now displayed enticingly on the shelves.

Without delay, Anna started to load her trolley. She bought almost the whole set of Enid Blyton's 'Famous Five' series for Shade, as she loved reading; some books about horses and dogs for Lola, who was passionate about animals; and some fairy tales for Femi, who was of an age to be read to and who enjoyed looking at the brightly coloured illustrations on every page, and identifying the people, animals and other objects that he recognised. Anna could not resist also picking up some new novels for herself in the adult section; reading about other people and places, particularly about England, did something to assuage her frequent feelings of alienation and homesickness.

When she had finished with the books, Anna turned to the toys, and picked out some dolls and soft toys, together with some jigsaws and board games. In the clothes section, she chose a couple of silk ties for Shola, one of his passions, and a jazz record which she knew he would like. Next she bought the Christmas decorations she needed, together with a bumper box of brightly coloured crackers, and some boxes of chocolates and cookies, as well as a Christmas pudding, which she really fancied herself. She often longed for the familiar foods of her own childhood, and when pregnant with Femi, had craved, of all improbable things, apple sauce. There were no fresh apples to be found in Jos at the time, so she had to resort to buying, and greedily consuming, the type sold in jars for babies.

Her trolley was now loaded; she would return for proper food shopping in a couple of days. In the meantime, she made her way to the checkout, with her trolley piled high. She might have felt guilty that she had scooped up so much Christmas booty, but she knew that if she did not grab what was there now, it would have disappeared by the time of her next visit.

Taking Chances

Her raid on Kingsway completed, and weighed down with bags and boxes, and followed by a store assistant with the heavier items, Anna made her way to her car, not forgetting to distribute a few meagre coins amongst the waiting beggars outside the store. She tipped the young man who had helped her, got into her car and drove home through the busy streets; she would have just enough time to hide the presents, before she had to be at school to pick up Shade and Lola. She decided that she would take Femi with her, and give Dorcas the rest of the day off.

❦

The next day was the date for the Carol Concert at Fairmount School, where Shade and Lola were pupils. The school had been originally set up for the children of American missionaries, carrying out their evangelical work in various parts of Africa, but it had been later opened to local children whose parents were able to afford the high fees. Many of the missionary children were boarders, but most of the others attended daily, like Shade and Lola. It had been a struggle getting the girls accepted into the school, as admission there was highly competitive, and the elite of Jos, black, white or mixed, local or expatriate, aspired for their children to attend this prestigious institution.

Anna had first heard about the school from Shade and Lola, as they had made friends with a little girl, whose Ugandan father worked at the university; her mother was French, and the child, Estelle, had been drawn to the two girls who were so similar to her in complexion, when they had all been living in university staff flats, prior to their move to the bungalow. Estelle attended Fairmount School, and had described it in such glowing terms to Shade and Lola that they had begged Shola and Anna to allow them to attend there also. There had been entrance exams and subsequently interviews, but eventually both girls had been admitted. They loved their school, and were both doing very well there.

Today was the last day of term. Shade and Lola were already at school, so Anna was going to attend the concert, taking Femi with her. Shola was busy elsewhere, so Anna would attend without him, and bring all the children back home when the concert was over.

Anna put on a smart dress and sandals; all the parents of children at Fairmount were well off, so she could not afford to appear too casually attired at this event. At the due time, she strapped Femi into his baby chair in the car, and set off for the school, which was located on the other side of the town, and at the top of a steep hill. When she was about half way there, Anna heard police sirens behind her, and pulled off the road just in time to allow a fleet of official cars to pass, accompanied by police on motor cycles. She had learnt her lesson the hard way. About two years previously, she had not heard the sirens, and when she finally was aware of them, she had not understood what they meant. When she eventually realised that she was expected to pull over and stop, she was accosted by a policeman, who remonstrated with her:

'Don't you know that is the military governor? You have insulted him by not moving out of the way. You have to come with me to the police station.'

At the time, Anna had the two girls with her in the car, and was expecting Femi. All three were shaking with fear, but the policeman, without further ado, climbed into the car beside Anna, and directed her to the main police station in the town.

When they arrived, she was instructed to get out of the car, with the children, and enter the police station. In this threatening environment, she was made to wait for about twenty minutes, before being ushered into the office of the chief of police. He was a thickset man, with kind eyes, which Anna thankfully spotted, behind his official grim expression. He reiterated what the other policeman had said.

Anna knew from experience, that to say 'sorry' expiated a multitude of sins in Nigeria. There was no use in blustering, as many expatriates did, when confronted with Nigerian authority, which most of them did not respect anyway. That always resulted in their getting into more trouble, which Anna privately thought, served them right for their arrogance.

Instead, she looked as if she was about to cry; she actually felt as if she might burst into tears at any moment. The two girls looked on anxiously.

'I'm really, really sorry,' quivered Anna. 'I didn't know what the sirens were for.'

'Where is your husband?' next demanded the police officer.

'He works at the university and I do, too. He is a senior lecturer in the English Department.'

'Is he Nigerian?'

'Yes, he's from Lagos.'

'Well, madame, I will let you go this time. We like people who like us,' he added cryptically. Anna guessed that this was a reference to the fact that her husband was Nigerian.

'You can go now. Don't do this again!'

Then the burly chief of police smiled; Anna could have hugged him.

'Thank you very much. I am truly very sorry.'

With that, Anna shepherded the girls back into her car, backed out of the police yard and drove away as fast as she could, without drawing further attention to herself.

※

When Anna reached the gates of Fairmount School, she swung her car into the drive that led through the extensive campus to the visitors' car park. The school buildings were attractively constructed, in a pleasing combination of brick and wood, and they included the main teaching blocks, the dormitories and a large chapel. All the buildings were flanked by leafy trees and grassy areas, providing a green calming environment, and there were numerous colourful flower beds, obviously tended and watered daily by the school gardeners.

In terms of religious affiliation, the school and of course, the chapel, were Christian and multidenominational; there was a strong Lutheran following as well as several other American non-conformist churches, such as Baptist and Presbyterian, which the missionaries represented.

Anna parked her car, unstrapped Femi, and carried him gently clasped in her arms, as she walked over to the school chapel. Many other parents were also arriving, and the chapel was already quite full. Anna found a seat about half way from the back, and at the end of an aisle in case Femi got restless. Once she was comfortably seated, she looked around her.

The simple modern chapel was decorated for Christmas with a beautiful Nativity tableau, displaying a multiracial group of figures: Mary, Joseph, the shepherds and the Three Wise Men, and of course the Baby Jesus, almost constructed to life size, took pride of place at the front, surrounded by fluffy white sheep and lambs. Angels, with gold haloes and enormous wings, flanked the group. A huge Christmas tree, decorated with ornaments and coloured lights, competed for attention at the side of the chapel, and the whole place sparkled and shone in anticipation both of the Carol Concert, and all the forthcoming Christmas festivities.

The parents sat attentively, waiting for the concert to begin. These parents represented every ethnic group in Nigeria, and also included a wide range of expatriates from many different countries. What they all had in common was the fact that they were members of the elite: they had money, good jobs and a high status in the society, whether by virtue of having the right connections or the right skin shade. Women in full Nigerian dress, wearing gold jewellery and rich brocades, sat beside British and American mothers, all dressed in their best for the occasion. There was a sprinkling of fathers, but most of the congregation were female, many of them, like Anna, accompanied by small children.

Taking Chances

Anna spotted one or two mothers she knew, and smiled and waved discreetly. Soon the concert started. Anna felt very proud to see both Shade and Lola appear with their respective classes, to sing carols for the delight of their audience of doting parents. When the children had performed, they were replaced at the front of the chapel by various American missionary teachers; some recited seasonal poetry; others sang, accompanying themselves on guitars. The men seemed all to have long hair and beards, and the women to be freckled and blonde. What they all seemed to share was an earnestness, and sincere Christian faith which they were endeavouring to impart, both to their pupils, and now their parents also. There was a brief address and blessing from a visiting American clergyman, and the concert was over. Parents and children were re-united, and the families made their way to their cars, amid laughter, happy shouts and excited chatter.

The next few days flew by for Anna, days filled with decorating the house, visiting Santa Claus at Kingsway, and going to the local market to purchase fresh fruit, vegetables, meat and fish. The children loved hanging the ornaments on the tree, the girls exclaiming with delight, and Femi watching wide-eyed, trying to reach out and touch the brightly coloured baubles, and having to be restrained by his vigilant sisters.

Soon Christmas Eve arrived. Anna eventually managed to get the excited children to bed, warning them that Santa Claus would not be able to come until they were fast asleep. Shola and Anna had their closest friends in Jos coming to visit: they were a Nigerian couple, George and Kemi, who lived on the same housing complex as they did, and who also had three children. Anna was very fond of Kemi, who was always ready to share an hour or two, chatting and exchanging their news and problems. George was also a senior lecturer at the university; he was in the Science faculty, a very mature man, highly respected by everyone who knew him, and a kind and reliable friend.

While she sat talking to Shola and their friends, all of them enjoying a glass of wine or beer, Anna busied herself in wrapping up the children's gifts in colourful Christmas paper, labelling them and placing them in their appropriate pillow cases, which they used for Christmas sacks. It was soothing, happy work, and she felt contented and at peace. At times like this, she was totally relaxed and optimistic about life in Nigeria, and could dismiss her fears as irrational and silly. Nothing bad would happen to any of them; it was Christmas and life was good.

CHAPTER FIVE

Three months later

One afternoon Anna was sitting in her office working on a lecture to be given the next day. She was so deep in the work, and lulled by the familiar gentle wheezing and purring of the air conditioner, that she was startled to hear the loud knock on her, door which was followed by Dorothy bursting into the room.

Dorothy had looked in a few times since the day when she first confided in Anna, and revealed how unhappy she was. Each time they had a coffee or soft drink together, and had mostly passed the time in small talk or sharing concerns about their children. Occasionally Anna caught a glimpse of Dorothy's red head and white face on the campus, standing out conspicuously in the crowd of African students, and then they would exchange a smile and a wave. Today, however, Anna could see immediately that there was a change in her friend. Dorothy was very pale and had obviously been crying; she was also trembling visibly.

'Come in and sit down. Can I get you a drink? What's the matter?'

'I don't want anything. I can't eat or sleep, and I don't think I can stay in that house another night.'

'What has happened?'

'Jide has brought a woman, one of those women who hang around the bar, into the house. He says she will be his second wife and that we should all be able to co-exist under one roof in traditional African fashion. Anna, what can I do? Please, please help me!'

Anna felt totally shocked and confused. Her immediate reaction was that she had to help Dorothy, but how?

'Look, we'd better sit down and talk about this. I will do my best to help but I can't make any promises, as I know that Shola will be against my 'interfering' as he puts it. I'll go and get us some coffee and we will try to figure something out'.

Over the next hour Anna and Dorothy discussed the situation. Dorothy told Anna that her parents, who lived in Liverpool, had always been supportive of her and her choice of husband. She was sure that even though they were not particularly well off, they would accommodate her and the children on a temporary basis if she could just make it back to the UK. Anna couldn't help silently comparing these unknown supportive parents with her own unsympathetic and narrow-minded ones.

'So do you want to go back home, or would you be prepared to stay on here if you can move out of Jide's house and support yourself and the children?'

'Well, I did think I would stay on, and that was my plan if I had got my degree. But now I can't do this as I haven't enough money to pay rent, support the children and continue as a student. I really don't have to option to stay, as I cannot possibly live in that house now that Jide has gone to these lengths. He is actually driving me mad.'

'So we will have to think of a way that you can leave the house immediately, without Jide suspecting that you are thinking of going to the UK. You need some kind of temporary refuge while we work on how to get you out of the country.'

While they had been talking, Anna had been wracking her brains to think of a solution. She knew it would be impossible to invite Dorothy to stay with them. Shola would not hear of it- he had already warned her not to get involved. In fact, she really could not discuss any of this with him. Suddenly she remembered an elderly American couple who had been very friendly towards her. She knew that they had a large house and were very hospitable. Professor Steiner taught Mathematics at the university and she occasionally ran into him and his wife at the staff club.

Anna visibly brightened as this idea took root in her mind. 'I've thought of a possible place for you to stay,' she exclaimed. 'We'll drive over to the Steiners. They are a really nice couple. Their children are all grown up, and live in the States. They might be able to put you up for a few weeks. You will have to tell Jide that they are renting you some accommodation, while you look for a cheap flat. You did say that he would not object to your moving out as long as you stayed in the area. Perhaps he has actually brought in this woman as a way of forcing you out. He must know that you would not stay in the circumstances.'

The Steiners had a large university bungalow on another campus, situated in the opposite side of the town, quite a distance away from the area where Anna lived. It was set in a secluded position, in a more established residential area than Anna's, having been built up some years earlier. The bungalow was surrounded by trees and bushes, pink and purple bougainvillea climbing to the roof and draping charmingly from trellises; brightly coloured flowers overflowed the attractive stone urns in which they were planted. A turbaned guard stood outside their gate, rather a scary figure in his black flowing garments, from which a sheathed sword protruded visibly, which marked him as being a member of a nomadic tribe from the north of the country. He was in fact a kindly man, who opened the gate to allow Anna and Dorothy access to the house.

The Steiners, themselves, were both of them thin, wiry, and grey-haired, Professor Steiner sporting a well trimmed grizzled beard. They had the kind of skin that many white people get, if they live a long time in the tropics, brown and a little dried out. Their bright blue eyes peeped out from sunken pale sockets, and they had similar expressions, in the way that many long married couples seemed to do. As individuals, they were extremely affable and unpretentious, and warm in a very American way. They were only too pleased to have Dorothy and the children to stay with them, once Anna had explained the situation.

'Sure they can stay,' they agreed. 'We'd love some young people around the house for a change!'

When things had been arranged, Anna dropped Dorothy at her house, returned to her office on the campus, and came back a couple of hours later. A flushed and red-eyed Dorothy emerged, carrying a few personal possessions in a couple of large leather bags, and the two little children. The children were obviously hot, bewildered and fretful, and whimpered on the back seat of the car, but they were greeted by the Steiners like long-lost grandchildren, and all three were soon settled. Anna left the three of them exploring their temporary sleeping accommodation.

Anna got home just in time to cook some supper and get the children to bed, trying to focus on what she was doing, despite her preoccupation with all that had happened in the past few hours. Later she struggled to appear normal and chatted to Shola as usual, but her mind was buzzing with the events of the day. She could not help feeling guilty at concealing everything that had occurred, but out of loyalty to Dorothy, and because she did not want a row, or to be expressly forbidden to have anything more to do with the situation, she had to keep quiet. She could not help having the quickly suppressed feeling that there must be something seriously wrong with her own marriage; the fact was painfully clear, even to her own woolly thinking, that she could not speak openly about all subjects to her husband, and that there were definitely 'no-go' topics.

※

Over the next few days Anna made a few brief visits to Dorothy at the Steiners. She dared not stay too long and arouse any kind of suspicion of her own involvement with Dorothy and her plans. Plans were in fact taking shape. The Steiners, Dorothy and Anna brainstormed ideas for how Dorothy could take the children back to the UK without being apprehended. They all agreed that it would be best for Dorothy to stay for at least a month with the Steiners so that Jide's fears, if he had any, that the children might be taken away, would be lulled. In fact, Dorothy should take them to see their father weekly, so that everything seemed to be normal. In the meantime, Dorothy would write to her parents and tell them that she would be coming to visit and requesting a loan to cover their airfares. Once she had the money, she would purchase air tickets, not travelling from the international airport at Kano which would be the obvious departure point to Europe from the north of the country. Instead, she would take an internal flight from Jos to Lagos, and then she would take an international flight from there; also she would book a flight on an Alitalia plane to Rome, and change there for an airline serving Manchester. Dorothy would have to dye her distinctive red hair a more neutral brown before leaving, to minimise the chance of being recognised by any of Jide's relatives, if they did in fact work at any of the airports or were on the lookout for her and the children.

※

A month passed and the day arrived for Dorothy's journey. Anna drove to the Steiners' house and picked up the three travellers, Dorothy looking pale and nervous, and unfamiliar with her newly acquired brown hair, the children fortunately oblivious to what was actually about to happen . She drove them and their small amount of luggage to Jos airport. The simple airport building was very small, but there was quite a long line of people queuing for the internal flight to Lagos. The queue was long and chaotic: women carrying children and large colourful items of hand luggage, and even pots of soup, jostled with business men sweating in European suits or wearing traditional Nigerian dress. Because the flight was only to an internal destination, the pre-flight checks were cursory. Anna hugged Dorothy and the children, and waved goodbye to the pathetic little group as they boarded the small Lagos-bound Nigeria Airways plane. As the flight took off, Anna prayed silently that they would survive the long and tortuous journey and arrive safely in the UK.

She felt tense and slightly feverish for the next week, worrying and wondering if they were safely in UK, or if they had somehow been stopped from boarding their flight in Lagos. Occasionally she drove, as unobtrusively as possible, past Jide's house, but could not see anything unusual going on.

About ten days after Dorothy's departure, in her customary way, Anna went to check her mail box at the university. Within it lay a postcard bearing a foreign stamp. She pounced on it greedily. Her hands trembling, she glimpsed through swimming eyes, the three words written on it: 'Made it. Thanks.' The postmark was Rome.

CHAPTER SIX

Ever since Dorothy's departure, Anna had been feeling slightly unwell, experiencing constant headaches and tiredness, which she assumed meant that she was going down with a cold. One morning about two weeks after she had received the postcard, she woke up with a throbbing pain in her head, slight nausea and all her limbs felt heavy and aching. She could barely get out of bed, so she asked Shola to drop the girls off at school, and said that she would go straight to the clinic, as there was no way she would be in any condition to go to work that day.

Dorcas was looking after Femi, and Anna decided that she would drive to the private clinic, where she had started taking the children following Femi's illness. However, her legs did not seem to be working properly and she could hardly stand. Sweat was pouring off her and yet she felt cold and clammy. She also felt afraid; her vision was blurred and she saw everything though a distorted prism of fever. She realised that she could not even attempt to drive herself, so she asked Dorcas to run quickly and call a neighbour. The neighbour, a friendly housewife, hurried over and after one look at Anna, immediately offered to take her to the clinic in her own car.

The trip to the clinic passed in a haze. Anna was alternately burning with fever or shivering uncontrollably; her head was pounding, and she could hardly see for the flashing lights before her eyes and the throbbing in her temples.

The private clinic, called the Star of Hope Hospital, was a marked contrast to the university clinic. It was situated in a quiet corner of the town. It had its own attractive courtyard containing palm trees and potted plants, and a comfortable waiting room, with easy chairs and glossy magazines on the central coffee table. The walls of the waiting room were adorned with carved wooden picture frames, containing soothing prints of seas, flowers and forests.

Anna was in no state to notice any of this on that day. She made it, with great difficulty, into the consulting room, supported by a nurse, and was helped to lie on the doctor's examination couch. The doctor, a very polite young Nigerian, named Dr Banjoko, examined her, looking grave. After a few checks of her temperature, pulse, mouth, he used a light to look into her eyes.

'Madame, I'm afraid that you have jaundice, which is known medically as hepatitis.'

'What does that mean?' croaked Anna.

'It means that you will have to rest in bed for several weeks, possibly a few months. It would be better if we admit you to the hospital so that you can be put on a glucose drip.'

'Please let me go home', she pleaded, terrified at the thought both of being alone in a strange hospital, where most patients would have relatives staying to look after them, and also of leaving the children with Shola. She knew from experience that he would be impatient, and possibly harsh with them, if she was not around.

'I'll let you go home on one condition: you will have to drink four large bottles of Lucozade each day, and you must keep it down, even if you feel nauseous. If you vomit, you must replace the liquid you lose as soon as you can. If you cannot do this, you will have to be admitted into the hospital, that is, if you want to survive. I will also treat you for malaria, as this accompanies any kind of illness in this country.'

Anna was driven back to her house, loaded with bottles of Lucozade and various medicines and pills. She had to be half carried into the house, and was barely conscious of how she eventually made it to her own bed. This was to be the beginning of a nightmare time, full of fear, pain and discomfort, where it was often difficult to know the difference between dreaming and reality

When she looked at her body, she was alarmed to see that her skin had turned a bright custard yellow. Every day and night she vomited repeatedly, shook with fever and found going to the bathroom an exhausting ordeal. She woke several times nightly, drenched in sweat. Shola usually slept through it all or pretended to. Shade played the role of a second mother to little Femi, who would howl miserably outside Anna's bedroom door, but could not be allowed inside in case he caught the virus. Her bedroom opened on to a corridor, but as well as a door, there was also a slatted window through which she could see her children outside her room. Her heart broke to hear her baby's sobs and Shade's efforts of comfort. Sometimes Anna feared that she would not ever recover and she would die, and be buried, in an alien and uncaring land, like the Biblical Ruth. She forced herself to drink the now disgusting Lucozade, and when she vomited it all up, she had to drink enough to replace it, and try to keep it down so that she did not have to go to the hospital. The only thing that kept alive her will to survive was the thought of the children. What would become of them if she should die?

Long days and weeks passed. Gradually the fever subsided and the vomiting stopped. Greta, a friend of Anna's, a German lady also married to a Nigerian, used to come to visit daily, and she would remake Anna's bed and help her to wash. Greta had three children and another on the way. She was short and blonde; her husband worked for a missionary organisation and her eldest daughter was Shade's closest friend at school. The whole family were committed Christians. Anna could never thank Greta enough, as without her help and encouragement she felt she might not have survived. Moreover, Greta was risking her own health to nurse Anna, showing a practical Christianity that was an inspiration compared with the hypocrisy of so many so-called religious people. Shola also used to encourage her and reassure that she would be alright, but he did little of practical help and kept his distance most of the time.

Shade was a wonderful support, and though only ten years old, would change Femi's nappies and generally look after him; Lola, being younger, usually seemed oblivious to what was happening, and got on with her own games and interests. As Anna started to regain some kind of appetite, Shade used to bake potatoes and bring these to Anna on a tray with pieces of fruit and other snacks.

While Anna lay in bed, day after day, she was at first too weak to read or do anything at all. Then, as she slowly felt better, she would lie and think and worry about the future both for herself and the children. Was it wise to stay here where it seemed that life was cheap and people could catch dangerous diseases and die so easily? Would Shola agree for the family to move back to the UK? Shade was now coming up to secondary school age. Wouldn't the children have more choices as adults if they were to be educated in Britain? Anna was coming to the conclusion that something would have to be resolved. She had started to feel disenchanted with life in Nigeria, not so much because she was afraid for her own health, but she was desperately worried about the fate of the children. Lola had always been a sickly child, having slight asthma as a baby and toddler, and she had recently complained continually of headaches. Perhaps she would be better in a cooler climate?

Anna decided that as soon as she was better she would have to put these things to Shola, and that together they would have to make a decision about their family's future. In her present weak state she felt depressed and fearful, but deep down she knew that it would be up to her to steer the family forward. It might be hard to convince Shola to see things her way, but she knew that since the death of his parents, as an only child, there was little to hold him in Nigeria.

She knew that things would be tough in Britain. They were always reading reports, or hearing news on the television, about job cuts under Thatcher's government, but somehow she felt sure that no matter how difficult, it would be better to be there. Anna's homesickness was now dictating her thought processes, and clouding her judgement. She had completely forgotten that she had been out of the UK for nearly ten years; she was seeing the country through an expatriate's rose tinted spectacles. She had also left Britain as a semi-child and would be returning as a mother of three. The country itself had changed under Margaret Thatcher, who had managed to bring out the worst in the British people. A culture of selfishness had been encouraged and only the strongest would prosper and thrive. Anna was unaware of any of these factors, and if they had been pointed out to her she would have dismissed them as exaggerated. She wanted to go home and nothing and no one would be able to dissuade her.

❦

Fortunately Anna managed to recover from her hepatitis after about six weeks, such a speedy recovery which even surprised her doctor. She lacked energy and everything was a major effort; however, she started back at work and gradually gained strength.

One evening she surprised Shola by bringing up the idea of their moving to the UK. She had expected him to be quite negative about the idea, at least in the first instance, and had envisaged a long and difficult campaign of persuasion. His career was going well and he was currently a senior lecturer. He would be up for reader within the next couple of years, and then it would only be a matter of time until he was professor. Amazingly, he was immediately keen on the idea of the move, having become disillusioned with his post, the university and the country in general. His jokes about 'Maggie's recessionals' as he had dubbed some of the expatriate British lecturers, was just a joke to them at this time. The reality behind this very apt description was largely lost on them, as potentially having any bearing on their own job search in Britain. Soon Anna and Shola were both applying for posts in the UK, spending hours of time and effort in their various speculative letters and formal applications.

They waited eagerly for replies to their applications, but all responses were negative, if the institutions or individuals bothered to respond at all. Some respondents even suggested that it was a waste of time to apply in the present state of unemployment in the country; others said that their applications would only be considered if they were actually in Britain. Perhaps they should have heeded the suggestions to be cautious, or to wait for a better time to go to Britain, but they were now both impatient to try out a new life and decided to take the plunge, with or without jobs to go to. All they needed to do was to raise some money and make their plans to travel from Nigeria to the UK with their young family. They were still young and naive enough to throw caution to the winds, trusting to their luck and determination to achieve their goals, despite the odds against them.

CHAPTER SEVEN

Over the next few weeks, Shola threw himself fully into preparing for the move. After his parents' death he had inherited their lives' savings, not amounting to much in the real world, but a tidy lump sum in the context of a university lecturer's salary. Shola had largely squandered this money, buying a new car, expensive furniture and financing a shopping trip to London for himself. Now he set about turning as many of their concrete assets as he could into cash. This had all to be done secretly as he did not want any hint of their plans to leak out at the university, as they had not formally resigned their posts.

Anna contacted her mother who reluctantly agreed to find them a rented house somewhere in Derbyshire, so that they would have a base from which to search for jobs once they were in the UK. All efforts to find jobs while they were still in Nigeria were now shelved, as it seemed impossible for achieve any positive results from so far away.

Shade and Lola were very excited at the idea of going to England; Femi was, of course, too young to understand what was going on. Anna was very concerned that none of the children had any winter clothes. She herself had only a light jacket for travelling, but hoped that the weather would not be too cold as they were planning to travel in the September of 1980. Shola, however, still had a number of suits and jackets, trophies from his earlier shopping expedition to London.

Anna felt sad at the idea of leaving her friends, especially Kemi and George, and her comfortable home. She also regretted having to take Shade and Lola out of Fairmount School, but she was now convinced, or had convinced herself, that they were making right choice. A few close friends knew about their plans, but were sworn to secrecy. Several of them, especially her best friend Kemi, warned Anna that they were taking a big risk, but she closed her ears to all advice. It was, of course, heart breaking to dispose of their birds – chickens, ducks and, of course, the grey African parrot, but it had to be done. They also had to sell or give away most of their personal possessions, such as books, records and ornaments, because they would only have a small baggage allowance. There was a constant stream of buyers, some interested in the birds, some in the records and books, and others in the furniture, coming in and out of the house. Soon the only thing left to dispose of was one car which would be collected on the last day.

Finally, the departure day arrived. They had chartered a large taxi to drive them to the Mallam Aminu Kano International airport in Kano State. The whole family piled into it at dawn, with as much luggage as would be permitted on the flight. The speed of the car on the uneven and bumpy roads alarmed Anna, but their driver, obviously accustomed to the route, drove on confidently, and in her opinion, recklessly. The children were all very quiet, sensing that they were embarking on a great adventure. As they descended from the plateau, the hotter air bathed them in its warmth, at first balmy, but soon overpowering. Even though they were limited in what they could take on the plane, the taxi was still loaded with possessions and soon everyone felt very uncomfortably hot and squashed. However, the excitement of the trip and their high hopes buoyed them up, and they were all thrilled to be finally approaching the airport and about to be on their way.

Kano was the third largest city in Nigeria, in terms of geographical size, after Lagos and Ibadan, which were both situated in the south of the country. It was the second most populous, after Lagos, and was very powerful politically, being the stronghold of the Hausa people, the largest single tribal group in the country. It was a predominantly Muslim city, and looking at the men walking about dressed in light coloured flowing robes, some in turbans, but all with some form of head covering, and the women all with headscarves, but many wearing veils, it might seem to the stranger, that they had suddenly found themselves in the Middle East. It might also feel intimidating to Nigerians from the Christian south of the country, especially if they remembered the slaughter of southerners in the north, which preceded the Biafra war, Nigeria's bloody and bitter civil war of the nineteen sixties. Now, the family looked out of the taxi windows at the city and people as they drove through, with fascination and awe.

The airport itself was hot and noisy. There were beggars outside, as well as traders displaying their carvings, and colourful hand woven mats and coverlets, to tempt departing expatriates. Loud voices haggled over prices in various Nigerian languages and pidgin English. Inside, it was all hustle and bustle, with people of all descriptions moving about, either trying to check in, or to tout for custom as porters, taxi drivers or to exchange currency. Men in Hausa attire mingled with Europeans and Africans in suits or casual wear, and women and children in their varied colourful costumes, filled the check-in area. The queue at the Nigeria Airways desk was loud and chaotic, with passengers and airport staff shouting at each other, as if about to come to blows, but fortunately as they were travelling by British Caledonian, they were able to avoid it. Their own queue, though quite long, was orderly and comparatively quiet. Anna, Shola and the children were relieved to hand their large and heavy suitcases to the clerk at the check-in, and be free to go and find somewhere to eat before their flight.

They soon found a cafeteria where they all had a choice of snacks and fizzy drinks. Unfortunately Shade decided to eat a salad, a choice that resulted in the poor girl being violently sick both in the airport toilet and on the plane, as well as suffering from excruciating stomach pains. Obviously the salad vegetables had not been washed or disinfected very thoroughly, and bacteria within them had attacked Shade's system with speed and ferocity. This did not get the family off to a very good start, with Anna feeling so concerned and worried about her daughter, and Shola getting increasingly irritated by the additional unnecessary complication.

'For heaven's sake,' he expostulated. 'It's the girl's own fault. I warned her not to eat that salad'. Shola had always disliked Shade, even though he would not admit it. He had resented her arrival, and the consequent shift in Anna's attention from himself to her first baby, and he still retained these hostile and negative feelings of jealousy.

Deep down both Shola and Anna were feeling very anxious about this adventure, even though they had mutually agreed to undertake it. They had abandoned secure jobs, a comfortable lifestyle and relatively high status in Nigerian society, to launch themselves and their family into the unknown. As this reality began to sink in, their subconscious tension showed itself in irritability and arguments.

They boarded the British Caledonian aircraft; the air conditioning on the plane chilled Anna and the children, wearing their light cotton clothing, as they settled into their seats. The smart airhostesses in their tartan uniforms, presented a sharp contrast to the chaos of the airport as they exuded an air of

Taking Chances

confidence and calm, which was at the same time reassuring and daunting. After years of being used to the rather relaxed and often annoying inefficiency of officials in Nigeria, Anna found these flaxen or red haired maidens very alien. She knew, however, that this was just the beginning. They were returning to a cold country with cold people, who might be more efficient and organised than the Nigerians, but they were lacking their warmth and heart.

❦

Arrival at Heathrow did indeed confirm Anna's fears about the coldness of Britain. As the family moved along the travelator, clutching their hand luggage, the cold and damp from outside seemed to penetrate the terminal building in some very insidious and threatening way. Anna carried Femi, clasping him tightly to her chest; Shola had the pushchair in one hand, and his other hand shepherded Lola in front of him. Shade walked close beside Anna, looking around her in wonder. It was an early morning in late September, and people around them were huddled in warm coats and jackets. Shola and Anna's little family shivered in light cardigans and thin shoes. 'I must buy the children some thick clothes as soon as I can,' Anna thought, inwardly panicking at the thought of one of them falling ill.

It seemed to take hours going through immigration. Anna and the children passed quite speedily through the British gate, but Shola was quizzed intensely by officials on why he was entering the country. Fortunately, he did have the appropriate visa and was eventually released to join the rest of the family. After they had waited ages to collect all their various pieces of luggage, they eventually found themselves spewed out of the terminal building and on to the underground railway station platform. Anna could smell the dampness all around and once again felt a sense of fear and panic about the future envelop her. Added to the physical chill, the headlines she had read on newspaper stands as they walked through the airport, about the latest murder victim of the Yorkshire Ripper, filled her with dread and apprehension. What kind of society had she brought her children into?

'We've got to get to Euston for our train to the north. I think we will have to change somewhere on the underground system,' Anna suggested. She realised that she would have to take the lead, as this was, after all her home country.

'We'd better get on this train and then ask someone,' Shola concurred.

Anna had never become familiar with London. She had visited there a few times years ago, but had usually been with other people who had known their way around. Now the responsibility of leading her family on this most challenging leg of their journey appalled her. Her stomach muscles clenched and unclenched as the full enormity of their situation loomed before her. She tried to appear confident for the sake of Shola and the children, but within she seethed with anxiety.

Eventually they found themselves at Euston, having taken directions from a helpful fellow passenger; the station seemed huge and confusing, with its various announcements about the arrival and departure of trains. A booming and unintelligible voice crackled out from somewhere above them, sounding like an alien from a science fiction movie, and they could not help but feel small and intimidated. Anna managed to locate a station official and asked about their train, and the family were subsequently directed to the correct platform, after they had purchased the appropriate tickets.

They soon found themselves on a long-distance train to Nottingham, from where they would have to find a taxi to take them to the small Derbyshire town that was their destination. Fortunately they were able to find a carriage containing relatively few passengers. The children were quiet, overwhelmed by all the new experiences that were happening to them. Anna had provided them with colouring books and crayons for the train journey and these kept the girls occupied. Femi slept peacefully oblivious in Anna's arms. They bought sandwiches and hot drinks when the trolley service came around, counting out the strange money uncertainly.

Decimalisation had happened when Anna was out of the country, so she felt even more out of her depth; she did not even understand the money system in the country where she had grown up. In fact, she felt a total stranger here. The country had altered in the years she had been away and she was now almost a foreigner; only the language was the same. Even the people looked different than she recalled from ten years earlier. She was glad to see that the passengers appeared to be a lot more ethnically mixed now, than they had been at the time she remembered, but it was still quite a shock to see all the changes that had happened without her awareness.

Shola and Anna said little to each other during the journey, both inwardly consumed by doubts and fears. How long would their meagre supply of money last? Would they be able to get jobs? Had they been totally foolhardy in this desperate enterprise? Anna felt guilty and responsible for everyone's safety and happiness. It had been her idea to come here; she must make it work for everyone's sake, and the sinking feeling inside her presaged a difficult time to come. A mere glance at the newspaper headlines confirmed that unemployment was rife, as job losses loomed large. So people who had warned them about the state of the British economy under Margaret Thatcher had been right. 'Please God, let us be alright,' breathed Anna silently, as their train sped them north into an uncertain future.

CHAPTER EIGHT

They soon settled into a little rented terrace house in the small Derbyshire town of Ashbourne, about thirteen miles from Derby. The town was situated in a very picturesque location adjacent to Dovedale and the surrounding limestone hills. It had become a tourist attraction from the eighteenth century, when many of its houses were re-built and its civic buildings augmented. The main street and market place were lined with fine looking Georgian houses, which gave the town a solid and prosperous feel.

Their own grey stone house, in a narrow street, was huddled between two similar ones on either side. It was a 'two up and two down' dwelling and was probably very much as it had been for the past two hundred years. They did have electricity and an indoor bathroom, but there was no central heating or any modern appliances. Anna and Shola shared their bedroom with Femi, while Shade and Lola had a small back bedroom for

Taking Chances

themselves. Any heating they had was provided by expensive to run electric stoves, and they used them as little as they could to keep the bills down.

Soggy grey skies, reflecting the shade of the grey stone houses, had now replaced the azure blue of their former West African home. Anna, feeling like the pauper she now was, managed to get the children and herself some warm clothes in the various charity shops dotted around the town. She began to get used to walking everywhere instead of driving her little car. She badly missed her yellow Volkswagon Igala, the Nigerian assembled hatchback car, which she had named Martha. In Jos she had enjoyed some status. There she had been seen as somebody, and the sort of somebody whom people respected and even envied. Now she was a complete nobody, and even worse, she was an undesirable nobody. People stared covertly and with disapproval as she wheeled Femi around the town in his pushchair, the girls on either side of her.

At this time Ashbourne was predominantly white; Anna could not remember seeing a single non-white face on her walks around the town. Sometimes she thought of Dorothy and wondered how she was getting on in Liverpool. Were she and her children facing similar isolation? Did she too experience hostility and discrimination? Anna, however, had no way of even knowing exactly where Dorothy lived, much less about how to get in touch. In fact, all that Anna could think of at this time was survival, her own and that of her family.

Shola had gone very quiet, a silence punctuated only with outbursts of irritability and anger, indicative of his natural anxiety and stress. Anna tried to pander to his every whim for the sake of peace, and also because she was very conscious of her responsibility in bringing about their present situation, making sure that he was regularly supplied with cigarettes, even though they were very short of money. He divided his time between applying frenetically for teaching jobs and watching television mindlessly. Anna applied for jobs too, but she also had to shop for food and other essentials and take the girls to school and pick them up afterwards.

She had managed to get both girls into the local primary school. This would be Shade's last year in primary, but Anna was hoping and praying that they would be settled by the time she was ready to move on to secondary school. The school was an unattractive bleak stone building, much the kind of primary school that Anna could remember attending some thirty years before, with few modern amenities. Both Shade and Lola hated it. As newcomers, and also as the only black children in the school, they were totally isolated. It was fortunate that they had each other to play with in the yard, as the other children eyed them with suspicion and often hostility. Frequently one or both of the girls would come home tearful having been labelled 'nigger' or 'wog'. They missed Fairmount, their privileged school back in Jos, where they had been part of the admired and elite mixed race group of children. Anna again felt terribly guilty for their present plight. She approached the head teacher at the school, and at least the name-calling stopped, but the girls were still seen as outsiders and not included in the other children's games.

Stress and worry about what the future might hold, and a terrible fear that her own selfishness had jeopardised the life chances of the whole family, started to take their toll on Anna. Her concentration was affected and she had two accidents within a couple of weeks. The first was merely slipping on an icy patch of pavement, while wheeling Femi in his pushchair; Anna fell heavily on her back, fortunately only suffering from painful bruising, shock and loss of dignity. The second accident was more serious.

Anna was out shopping on her own, but she was rushing to get back home, as she knew Shola resented being left alone to babysit Femi for too long. She simply did not notice a series of bollards at the side of the pavement, and walked heavily and rapidly into one. The pain in her chest was excruciating, and she doubled up, falling to the ground in agony. The shop keeper and his assistants from a nearby store rushed out to help her, and she was supported into the shop and put into a chair. The pain was intolerable and Anna could not suppress her groans; hot tears fell from her eyes unchecked, as she was being comforted by the shop assistants. An ambulance was summoned and Anna found herself in Casualty.

After an x-ray, Anna was told that she had two cracked ribs, but that nothing could be done except to take painkillers, while the ribs healed on their own. She was taken home, supplied with tablets, and instructed to rest. Rest was really out of the question, as she had the children to look after, food to buy and cook, and generally to keep the family going. Sleep was very difficult as she was unable to lie down, and had to doze, propped up on pillows in their cold bedroom; she endured this torture, feeling that it was a just punishment for her past mistakes. Eventually the intensity of the pain subsided, but the niggling pain in her chest remained with her for many months, like a physical manifestation of her intense mental pangs of anxiety.

※

One day, a few weeks later, a letter arrived for Anna by first class mail. She opened it hesitantly, but hoping it would contain something positive, as rejection letters tended to be sent by second class. It was what she had been longing for, a brief letter inviting her for an interview for a teaching post at a comprehensive school in Derby. This would be the first interview to which she had been called since she had started applying for jobs in Derbyshire. Anna felt both excited and nervous as they badly needed for at least one of them to get work; their savings were dwindling and they were reluctant to apply for unemployment benefits.

When Anna arrived at the school for her interview, the head master, a grey-haired man of middle age, was very friendly and affable.

'How do you do, Mrs Banjo? I hope you won't be offended by this, but I was expecting an African, er black lady.'

'Oh,' said Anna, a little taken aback. 'Were you hoping for a black person to fill the post?'

'Well actually, I was. You see, we have large number of ethnic minority pupils in this school and only one Asian teacher and one West Indian. I was hoping that we might recruit another non-white teacher as a role model for our children.'

Anna's spirits actually soared. 'Well, you don't need me, you need my husband. He is also an English teacher. He even has a Ph.D. from Manchester University.'

'Would he be interested in this job? It is only a temporary post as a main grade teacher.'

'I'm sure he would be interested. If it is alright with you I will go home now and perhaps he could come and see you tomorrow.'

'That would be very good. I'll expect him at ten tomorrow morning.'

Anna raced home to tell Shola the wonderful news. She mentally urged on the infuriatingly slow and wheezy bus the thirteen long miles back to Ashbourne. She had realised all along that it would probably be easier for her to get a job than for Shola because she was white, but now in fact it seemed that his blackness might, for once, be an advantage. Anna was so glad to be the bearer of good tidings and she knew how relieved Shola would be to have a job. She had felt instinctively that he would hate it if she had been the first to find work, leaving him at home unemployed, even if they had been offered no choice through financial necessity.

Shola was very excited at the news. The next morning, dressed in a freshly ironed shirt, tie and suit, with shiny polished shoes, he set off for Derby. It was soon arranged and Shola started work at he beginning of the following month.

It was by this time almost Christmas. Anna managed to purchase some small gifts for the children, which she wrapped up in Christmas paper so that they would have the fun of opening their presents on Christmas day just as they had done in Nigeria. Of course, the gifts were smaller and less expensive, but at least they could carry out the ritual of unwrapping and exclaiming over their new toys and books. She could not help thinking back regretfully to their last warm and happy Christmas in Jos, especially Christmas Eve, spent with their friends, Kemi and George, in their comfortable university bungalow.

The house in Ashbourne was never really warm enough. They could only afford to heat the main room, and bathing and going up to bed were something of an ordeal. Anna, herself shivering, though wrapped up in as many sweaters as she could manage, would have to supervise the lukewarm baths of the protesting children each night, and bundle them into hot water bottle heated beds as quickly as she could. However, now that Shola was working there would be money to pay the bills and they hoped that things would get easier.

Anna continued to apply for jobs and in early March, she had an interview for a temporary job teaching English to Vietnamese refugees at a reception centre in Derby. She got the job and also made friends with the lecturer in charge of the teaching at the centre. Alison, coming from an educated middleclass background, was married to a West Indian teacher who coincidentally taught at the same school as Shola, so they had quite a lot in common. The two couples became friends, and Anna and Shola, with the children, would sometimes visit Alison and Ellis in their comfortable home in Derby, with its modern kitchen, light and airy living room and large and leafy green garden.

Anna was able to take Femi with her to work as the centre had a crèche for the Vietnamese children, while their parents had English lessons. She was able to spend time with him in her breaks and make sure that he had a good lunch along with her. Anna experienced the teaching in the centre as both challenging and rewarding. She found herself on some occasions, teaching one to one, a Vietnamese adult with absolutely no English, sometimes a person even illiterate in their own language. It amazed her that after a morning together, she and her student would have communicated interesting facts about their respective families, while her student would have picked up some basic and simple English words. She enjoyed her work and was sorry that her post was only a temporary one, as the centre would soon be closing down when the last of the refugees were settled in their own housing.

❦

The months passed and summer arrived. Both temporary jobs were coming to an end. They must find something else. Shola applied for a post at a further education centre in Liverpool. This centre had been set up by the members of the mixed race community to serve principally their own people. Shola was recruited to teach Black History. There had been riots in Liverpool that summer, which had even prompted a visit to the city from Margaret Thatcher's then Secretary of State for the Environment, Michael Heseltine. Now efforts were being made, rather belatedly, to improve race relations in the city and this included providing better educational opportunities for young black people.

Although he was really a teacher of English, Shola was delighted to have the opportunity to study a new and relevant subject area, and to be able to teach the students about important figures in Black history, such as Marcus Garvey and Malcolm X. He was very excited about the job. Now all they had to do was to find a place to live in Merseyside and move the family.

Anna was filled with hope that they would be able to settle and have a better life. It was time for Shade to start secondary school, and she prayed that they would be able to afford to send all the children to private schools, in the hope and expectation that they would thereby be able to avoid at least the cruder forms of racism from their fellow pupils.

Taking Chances

Anna started to apply for jobs in Liverpool, and eventually was offered a post on the supply team to teach in Knowsley, a predominantly white working class area in north Liverpool. She did not feel particularly happy or optimistic about this, but they needed the money, so she had little choice. At least they were moving on; they both had jobs and they might at last have a permanent home.

Knowing nothing of Merseyside, they found a house to rent in the town of Birkenhead, just across the river from the centre of Liverpool. This was to prove a costly mistake as the area where the house was situated was almost completely white and very racist. Shola and Anna were totally ignorant and unaware of this factor in their choice of location, but it was to be a source of unhappiness and trauma for the whole family, especially the children.

CHAPTER NINE

The move to Merseyside was a terrible mistake. Though their time in Derbyshire had been an anxious one, with the uncertainty about money and employment, they had been basically full of hope about a change for the better, and while they had encountered unfriendly looks from some people on the streets of Ashbourne, Derby had been quite racially mixed and much more tolerant in their personal experience. Now they were to encounter overt hostility and animosity, and their unknowing choice of a white working class area as their new home was one of the worst decisions of their lives.

Birkenhead, where they were to live, was a town on the Wirral Peninsular, and was situated on the west bank of the River Mersey, directly across the river from Liverpool. An underground railway tunnel, running under the Mersey, linked the town with Liverpool, as well as a road tunnel named Queensway. Before either of these options existed for travel between

Taking Chances

Birkenhead and Liverpool, there was a ferry over the river, made famous in the song 'Ferry cross the Mersey' by Gerry and the Pacemakers in the sixties. The ferry was still in operation, and it made a pleasant travel alternative if the weather was good and one was not in a hurry. Occasionally the ferry trip was compulsory, when there was industrial action on the railways. Then commuters would throng the decks, and the obligatory playing of the famous song, would emanate incongruously from the speakers, sounding tinny and clichéd to the packed workers, anxious about being late to their office or shop.

Many residents of Birkenhead commuted to jobs in Liverpool, if they were fortunate enough to have any kind of employment. The town had been famous for its shipbuilding industry since the early nineteenth century, and Cammell Laird's ship yard had been the main employer since then. However, at the time when Anna and Shola arrived in Birkenhead with their family, the ship yard was in decline, and most of its former employees were on the dole. Birkenhead was now a sullen and resentful town, rather than a hive of activity that it had been in the past.

Margaret Thatcher's economic policies, and her ideology that there 'was no such thing as society', had combined to bring about mass unemployment across the whole country, and Merseyside had been particularly badly hit. Both Liverpool and Birkenhead were tragic victims of the recession, and with the decline of the north's manufacturing bases, whole families were on benefits, with no promise of any male in the family ever being employed again. Sometimes women could find part-time jobs in service industries, but the masculine brute strength that used to be required in construction and industrial work, was no longer in demand. Men would sit around in their houses all day, drinking alcohol if they could get their hands on it, while women would work for a pittance cleaning or serving in shops, and then be expected to clear up the mess in their homes when they returned from work. Domestic violence was on the increase, and frustration and despair oozed out onto the street corners and into the pubs and clubs. Petty crime was the order of the day, as people became desperate to lay their hands on money, by any means they could devise.

It was into this social and economic scenario that Anna and Shola had brought their young family. Their rented house was situated on an upper working class estate in a suburb named Noctorum, about two miles from the underground station in Hamilton Square, which was the closest station to the river, and beyond to Liverpool. The house itself was the type that Anna would always think of as a 'box house'. Built about fifteen years previously, it stood in a very large development of similar looking, cheaply built houses. There was some differentiation in terms of roof shapes – some had sloping chalet type roofs with flat extensions over the top floor front windows; others were built in traditional style – but overall there was a sense of sameness about the location. The houses were mostly semi-detached with gardens front and back. Most of the houses were well looked after, and their owners lovingly added features, such as porches and conservatories, doing their DIY at the weekends. The gardens were also well tended, with neat front lawns, shrubs and the occasional weeping cherry. Sundays would see residents weeding and mowing their pocket handkerchief sized lawns with much diligence and commitment.

Despite all this human care and activity, the place always felt cold, like a disapproving host of evacuees, to Anna and her family: they felt excluded and alien, and were aware of being seen as such by the other inhabitants of the area. Nevertheless, the houses themselves were functional if cramped, with two medium sized bedrooms and one additional tiny one, just large enough to accommodate a single bed. The front sitting rooms were open plan with stairs leading upstairs directly from them, while the kitchens were located at the back with a door leading out into the back garden. Most of the local people were young upper working class families with small children, though there were also some retired couples. Almost without exception, these people exuded an air of smug satisfaction that they were house-owners, in a financial position to pay a mortgage, and had escaped from the council estates of their childhood. This was more pronounced because of the prevailing unemployment in Merseyside. The majority of the men were skilled, and often self-employed, plumbers and joiners, who had not been condemned to the despair of the dole queues which their less fortunate school mates were enduring in the Thatcher years.

This estate was to be Anna and her family's home for the next ten years. For the first couple of years they lived in their rented house, and then managed to get a mortgage to buy a similar one a few roads away, because it was on the market at a low price. Anna looked back at this period of her life as one long nightmarish drudge. Every time she wanted to break down and weep, long having regretted the move from Nigeria, she had to keep it bottled inside; it had been at her instigation that they had got into this place and situation. She could not admit either to herself or to Shola that it had been an almost criminal error. She could see after only a few months that their plight was taking its toll on the whole family, but she was not wise enough to realise that it was not something that could somehow work out right in time. A human ostrich, she kept her head in the sand because she could not face the consequences of her own selfish and ignorant decision, and she had no idea how they would be able to reverse it.' Somehow,' she told herself,' things will get better.' Optimism had always been one of Anna's strengths, but now it was a deluded weakness.

Shola and Anna decided that the children must go to private schools, no matter what the cost. After the girls' experiences in the school in Ashbourne, they did not want them to be subjected to the overt racism of the state education system. They were, after all, living in an all white working class area of Merseyside, and even they, in their comparative ignorance, knew that their children would be condemned to a living hell if they were sent to the local state schools.

Shade took the entrance test to a private girls' school in Liverpool and was accepted after an interview. It was decided that she would travel by bus and train from Birkenhead to Liverpool each day with Anna, who would be on her way to work in Knowsley. Lola would attend a preparatory school which was only a short bus ride away from where they lived, and would be joined there by Femi when he reached the age of three. They would be escorted to school by Shola, and he would then travel on to Liverpool also.

Until Femi was old enough to attend school, and even later on when he needed to be collected from his junior school before the rest of the family came home, he was looked after by a child minder. Millie, short for Mildred, was part of their lives over several years. Millie lived close by in a rather better house than Anna's. Her house was detached, with a well tended garden and several shady trees to give it some character, and it was situated about five minutes' walk away from Anna's road. She and her husband had one adopted daughter a little younger than Lola, whose room was furnished like that of a princess, all pink frills and dreamy bed covers and curtains.

Millie was never tired of telling Anna that she came from a slightly higher class family than her husband, and she used to enunciate her words in a very precise upper class accent which was obviously assumed. She was, however, a large jolly woman, with a very good heart. She had blonde wavy hair, and she liked to wear huge caftans in an attempt to hide her girth, but this was an impossible task, and her belly was always clearly visible beneath the folds of her loose garments. In shape she reminded Anna of the Tenniel drawings of the Duchess in 'Alice in Wonderland' which she had seen as a child, or a fat merry Buddha. When she laughed, the rolls of fat shook and tears of mirth would flow from her eyes. She would be one of Anna's only friends for several years, and although her behaviour was erratic, and from an objective viewpoint she was quite a sad and comical figure, she remained a constant in their lives. They kept

Taking Chances

in touch even after Femi was too big for a child minder and to some extent shared each other's ongoing struggles with life.

Anna's working days were long, exhausting and relentless. She would be up before six to prepare breakfast, packed lunches, and bus money for the children. She had also to ensure that they had clean underwear and school uniforms, and any other necessities that they required for school. This was just about manageable if the children were well, but if one of them was sick then she would have to make complicated arrangements for their care, or call in sick herself. When she had travelled home by train and bus, collected the children from school, cooked supper for everyone and got the children to bed, she used to collapse into an almost drugged sleep, to prepare herself for a dreary repeat performance the next day. In the winter months, she would be up in the dark, home in the dark, and it felt as if she was herself in some dark tunnel without any prospect of light at the end. Both she and Shola were too shattered at the end of their respective days to communicate, and both were wrapped in their own little worlds of despair.

Shola's job at the education centre was not too bad, but there was continual in-fighting between different factions, and his position was far from secure. The tension was mainly between the Liverpool-born members of staff, and the African lecturers, who were not even united among themselves. He was paid no superannuation, and was very conscious that he would have to get a better paid and safer job as soon as he could. He could not help comparing his present lot to his position in Nigeria, as an up and coming senior lecturer with professorship around the corner.

However, compared to Anna's situation, Shola's job was heaven. Anna lived in a kind of purgatory, and she felt that she must be expiating heinous sins of the past to be subjected to such on-going misery. Her job was as a supply teacher of English, and she was employed by the north Liverpool borough of Knowsley. As such she would be placed in a comprehensive school to cover long term leave such as maternity or serious illness. Her placements were usually for a minimum of one year. The main problem of this arrangement was that the regular staff tended to see her as an outsider and as such, slightly beneath them; and the children too, soon worked out that she was not a 'proper' member of staff and was therefore fair game for bad behaviour, and teacher baiting. Added to this, her name, Mrs Banjo, allowed much scope for miming and name calling, if the culprits were in a crowd and therefore felt safe from positive identification. Being on 'yard duty' was rather like being thrown to the lions in a Roman circus, and Anna was never sure whether she would survive break time, without having a missile thrown at her head from some unseen hand. Sometimes she would have to go into the girls' toilet to flush out smokers, and she dreaded the whispered insults that the girls would automatically hiss, and then deny uttering.

Anna soon learned that the key to survival in this system was not to be a great teacher, but to assume the role and persona of prison warder. After the torture of her first placement, she hardened herself mentally and emotionally, and learned to feel satisfied if she managed to keep her classes under some form of control, and that most of her pupils had at least written a page in their exercise books by the end of the lesson. But it was wearing day after day to have to intercept flying pencils and pieces of paper; to refer children to their year heads for punishment; and sometimes to keep children behind after school as a form of discipline. Anna always felt that this was punishment for her rather than the offenders, as she worried about her own children when she came home later than usual.

She came to thoroughly identify with D. H. Lawrence's feelings in his poem, 'Last Lesson of the Afternoon', with its famous opening line, 'When will the bell ring, and end this weariness?' Anna was far from the only teacher to be under stress; on the contrary, the more human and sensitive teachers were all vulnerable. The staffrooms would billow forth smoke at break time, and haggard teachers would be seen hurrying in with books under their arms, struggling to light a cigarette before they had even found a place to sit down.

These schools were largely battle grounds, where small battalions of lower middle class teachers struggled to tame and educate armies of the children of the under class – the mass unemployed and increasingly unemployable inhabitants of the white council estate ghettoes of the area, casualties of the Thatcher years. A few of these children would be successful and go on to college, but the majority would repeat the lives of their parents and themselves join the ranks of the unemployed. Anna used sometimes to exhort her pupils to work hard, so that they could get jobs when they left school. They would often laugh derisively, and cite relatives of their own who had a clutch of O levels, but were out of work nevertheless. Why should they try, they would say, when the result would be the same? It was difficult to argue with such logic, though Anna used to try. After all, she was well educated, and yet she was here, as a supply teacher, working on a sink estate as it was the only job available to her. This was Thatcher's Britain, and Anna had only herself to blame that she had become trapped there.

Reading was her only pleasure. On her journeys to and from work, on the long tedious bus rides through Liverpool to Knowsley, she consumed novel after novel. These books conveyed her to another world, and though she would have been hard put to it to remember any details of their content a month later, they had a way of soothing her. Perhaps her plight was universal: other women had been in despair and pain, but they had triumphed over adversity eventually. Maybe she would too.

Helen Forrester's autobiographical 'Twopence to Cross the Mersey,' and its sequels, in which the author described her early life of tremendous hardship growing up in Liverpool, and how through her own tenacity and determination to survive, she finally achieved acceptance and success, Anna found particularly inspirational. But her books could not alleviate the frequent feelings of physical sickness which came flooding over her, when her bus approached the school bus stop at the beginning of a new day of torture.

Anna's preoccupation with her own plight obscured her perception of her own children's struggles. Shade was lonely and isolated at school. The school was a traditional fee paying girls' high school, and most of its pupils were from middle class backgrounds, their families living in the leafy affluent suburbs of Liverpool, largely unaffected by the unemployment and poverty of other areas of the city. The headmistress was a pearly middle aged spinster, with an affected voice, who sounded a bit like the queen when she spoke. She was cool and condescending to Anna, professionally polite and concerned, but quite detached from the real world in which Anna and Shade lived. Because Shade had started the school year a little late, the other girls had already formed their own friendship groups, by the time she joined her class. Added to this she was one of only a few non-white girls in the school so she was visibly different to most of her class; the only other mixed race girl had been grudgingly accepted into a peer group, and was not interested in risking her own tenuous position to try to include Shade. At lunch time, Shade would wander round on her own, conspicuous because she was alone and black, and unsure of what she should do. She was often teased by the class bullies, and found her experience of her school even more traumatic than Anna's suffering in her teaching role.

Lola, and Femi, who at three had joined the nursery class, of a private preparatory school, experienced some name calling and other forms of bullying, but this stopped after Anna complained to the head mistress of the school. She was much more approachable and sympathetic than Shade's headmistress, and did not want any unpleasantness in her school; she also strongly believed that school should be a positive experience for all her pupils. She was quick to warn all those concerned that she would take serious action if there was any repetition of the bullying, and her firm stance fortunately prevented any recurrence of the racist incidents. But of course there were underlying prejudices among both staff and pupils, which showed themselves in less overt, but none the less distressing manifestations.

All members of the family were enduring emotional anguish on their own, and each was alone in their isolated and private suffering. Furthermore, because of all the pressures they faced individually, they were unable to console and support each other. As in a pressure cooker, the steam would have to escape eventually, and over the next weeks and months and years, the build up of frustration and tension would manifest itself in increasingly disturbing ways.

CHAPTER TEN

Shola had always had a volatile temper. Even in their early days together Anna had been alarmed at how quickly he could become angry and potentially violent; it only took someone accidentally spilling his drink in a bar or looking at him in the wrong way, to trigger an ugly scene. Anna would find these incidents excruciating and would try to disentangle Shola, and extricate them both from the situation, but usually to no avail. Shola had to feel that he had 'won' and would revisit the conflict verbally for hours afterwards, loudly emphatic that he had been in the right. Anna always felt disturbed and frightened by these episodes, but then Shola would return to being his charming self, and she would suppress her fears until the next outbreak.

Now his mood swings became increasingly unpredictable and alarming. One day he could come home from work happy and jovial, handing out chocolate bars and other goodies to the children; on another day he would storm into the house, his face contorted with aggression, barking out orders to both Anna and the children, and they would live in dread of what the evening would bring. Weekends, too, could become a nightmare with Shola terrorising the family with his whims and outbursts, and woe betide anyone who failed to conform and obey instantly.

Underlying many of these episodes were Shola's frustrations with life in Britain, particularly with his job, and also his fear that he was losing his identity as a Nigerian, and that his children were not being raised the 'African' way. He became ever more obsessive, even manic, about the children eating Nigerian food, doing the housework and being 'seen and not heard.' Any perceived or imagined infraction of his rules would be met with a frightening, and possibly violent, reaction.

Occasionally he would force Anna to wake the children at five in the morning to come down for 'prayers.' When he could not be dissuaded, she would go up and wake the poor things, afraid that if she did not do this gently, in her own way, he would do so in a very brutal way. The three children would descend the stairs, yawning and rubbing their eyes, doing their best to conform to their father's demands. At other times, he would make an issue of the Nigerian food. He would demand that Anna made okra soup, and that the children, particularly the two girls, would have to eat it.

'You will eat,' he would roar, his eyes flashing dangerously. Anna and the children would cringe, and prepare for a terrifying ordeal to come.

Okra soup, prepared the African way, has a very viscous consistency, and for children who had not been used to eating it from a very young age, it could seem unappetising or even revolting. Moreover, Shola, oblivious to any element of child psychology, used to command them to eat, as if it was a punishment, which of course it became in their eyes. Anna used to give them only tiny portions, and tried to encourage them to eat it, cajoling or even bribing them to conform to their father's wishes. Often, when all persuasion failed, she used to either eat their portions herself, or surreptitiously dispose of the food.

However, if Shola caught them out, he would force them to eat the food in front of him. If they could not, or gagged, he would beat them with his leather belt, in an almost ritualistic performance, which seemed to give him a perverse pleasure.

'I will give you ten strokes!' he would shout, glorying in the terror and agony, mental and physical, he was inflicting.

He used to pick on Shade in a particularly vindictive way, both to humiliate her and give her pain. Whenever he had complaints about the children, he used to always add 'Particularly that Shade,' as a way of identifying her as the main culprit. He had always resented and been jealous of Anna's close relationship with her, and used to vent all his myriad frustrations on the poor little girl. The other two children would look on in fear and compassion for their sister, but there was nothing they could do. Once when Lola protested, she too was subjected to a beating.

In truth, Shola found being a father an impossible task. On the surface, he conformed to the African ideal of desiring a family, but inside he was still a child himself. He was jealous of Anna's involvement with the children, wanting all her time and attention for himself; he punished the children, not so much for any misdemeanour, but for actually being there.

In later years Anna looked back and wondered why she had not stood up to Shola at this time, or even left him. Instead she acted like a frightened rabbit caught in the headlights of a car: she froze. It was true to say that she was confused. Her nature was not punitive, so she felt naturally horrified and revolted by his words and actions, but on the other hand, she feared that she was looking at all this from a very European viewpoint – perhaps Shola was just doing what he thought was right as an African parent. What could she do? She was conscious that she had encouraged Shola to leave his own country, and felt a kind of loyalty and duty towards him in this alien land. She also feared the violence of his reaction if she did try to leave him, or even called in outside assistance. What if he either killed one of the children, which he occasionally threatened to do, or even went off with Femi, as he was still too young to understand what was going on? Would he carry out any of his terrifying threats? Anna was too scared to take the chance.

She could, of course, if she had possessed sufficient determination and courage, have turned to the authorities: the police or the social services, but her pride, and her reluctance to 'betray' Shola to the racist agents of the state, as well as her fear of a tragedy occurring before they could actually be helped, continually held her back.

When Shola was not at home terrorising the family, he would stay out late in Liverpool. There he would frequent the clubs and pubs of Toxteth, a black ghetto of the city, getting drunk and smoking cannabis with drinking buddies and acquaintances, in an attempt to forget his grievances and disappointments. If Anna made the mistake of asking him why he was so late home, he would react violently, often hurling the food she had kept for him at the wall. She learnt to keep quiet and to actually relish the peace of the home when he was out.

The only times that Shola was himself peaceful in the house were when he lay on the sofa watching television or videos; when he was doing his ironing, accompanied by his records on at full blast; or when he fell asleep in a cannabis-induced stupor. Sometimes, if he was in an expansive mood, he would urge the children to join him in watching horror movies, which terrified them, and Anna used to discourage this activity in a tactful way, if she could.

The most harmonious times were when Shola was tending his garden, which he genuinely enjoyed. He used to cultivate vegetables and fruit, and would often spend hours in the garden, perfectly happy and at peace. Growing plants seemed to calm and satisfy him, but he had no time for flowers, because they were not functional, but merely frivolous in his view. He loved to come in from the garden with handfuls of fresh produce, such as tomatoes, cucumbers and soft fruit, which he proudly presented to Anna. She used to chat to him, and help with the gardening chores, and momentarily forget the bad side of their life together.

For Anna work was hell, life at home was often hell, but even going out food shopping, or using the launderette, could also be a humiliating and traumatic experience. They could not afford a car at this time, so they had to travel by public transport, and in the early years they could not even afford a washing machine. This meant that while Femi was still small they would have to take the pushchair on the bus, as well as their bags of washing, or when they went shopping, they had to return on a crowded bus with all their shopping bags, and the awkward and unwieldy pushchair.

Sometimes they would return home by taxi. Anna used a false name for the purpose of getting taxis. She had learnt to do this the hard way. On the first occasion when she called a Birkenhead taxi, using the name Mrs Banjo, the taxi failed to turn up. Anna phoned the company again. 'I called for a taxi over half an hour ago. Why hasn't it arrived yet?' she demanded.

There was a silence at the other end of the line. Then a thick Merseyside male voice replied, 'We thought youse was joking.'

After this Anna always used the name 'Bancroft' when communicating with the taxi office, to ensure that a taxi actually turned up.

Usually, Anna would make these trips on her own with the children. On some occasions she would be verbally abused or mocked. In Birkenhead market, bustling with seething humanity, but full of cheap and affordable items, she was shocked and shamed to be abused by the men on the smelly butchers counters, being called 'whore' and other similar epithets. After this, she avoided that side of the market, but the abuse could come from any unexpected quarter. She tried to protect the children from awareness of this abuse as much

Taking Chances

as possible, but inevitably they absorbed the hostile atmosphere more and more as they grew up, and started to understand the dynamics of their environment.

Birkenhead at this period was extremely and notoriously racist. When they told other black people in Liverpool about where they lived, these people were shocked that they had not known about the Wirral town's reputation. Liverpool blacks did not live in or even visit Birkenhead. In fact, not only Birkenhead, but the whole of Merseyside was rife with racism. Anna heard stories of how black people living in Liverpool, who had innocently found themselves in localities outside of the black ghetto of Toxteth, were invariably told by the police, in no uncertain terms, to get back to their own area.

Even when she did not receive actual verbal abuse, Anna was conscious of the hostile eyes on her and the children as they walked round the town centre, and of course their own residential area. Later as the children got older and would travel home from school by bus on their own, they would be called racist names as they walked through the estate, after a long day at school. They would tearfully tell Anna about it, asking why these people acted in this way. Her heart would break within her, but all she could say was 'They're ignorant. Just ignore them.' Not much help to her miserable children.

※

After a couple of years, Lola joined Shade at her school in Liverpool. Now the two girls travelled to school and back together by bus and train, a long and tedious journey. Lola often fell asleep on the bus on their return trip, but Shade equally exhausted, but as the elder, vigilant and responsible, ensured their safe arrival home. Femi remained at his preparatory school in Birkenhead, escorted to school by Anna, before her long trek through Liverpool. Millie would pick him up from school and keep him with her until Anna got home from work. Anna would sometimes sit down for a cup of tea with Millie; it was a comfort to have someone to confide in.

'My Tom used to get called names at school. He's dark as a gypsy,' Millie told her one day, when she was complaining about the racism the children were experiencing. Tom was indeed of a swarthy complexion, but certainly white. Millie used to chortle away, no matter what the topic of conversation, and Anna could not help but feel better to be able to lighten her mood, and even laugh with a friendly person. Millie's adopted daughter was of an Italian background, apparently matched with Millie and Tom on account of Tom's dark skin tone.

Millie used to tease Femi, if Anna was late in picking him up. 'Perhaps your mother's run off with a Chinaman!' she would giggle.

Millie was very good-natured, if garrulous. She was studying for an Open University degree, and used sometimes to discuss the books she was reading and her essays with Anna. Millie was herself something of an unpredictable character: she would usually be very sedate, and very ladylike. She would enunciate her words with care as if she were in an elocution lesson. She told Anna that she was born in Formby, a posh area of Merseyside, and that she could have married very well. Instead she married dark skinned Tom, apparently much to the chagrin of her parents. However, on some occasions she would totally change, and become a very different person.

One day, Femi came running home minutes after Anna had dropped him off at Millie's house.

'Mummy, Millie said I should come home. She's having a terrible row with Tom, and I was really scared.'

Next time Anna saw Millie this incident was not discussed, but thereafter Anna did not feel inhibited about confiding in Millie after some of her own domestic dramas. In fact, it was Millie's house that Anna and the children sought as a refuge, after particularly ugly conflicts in their own home.

Taking Chances

On one occasion, after a violent row, they had left their house and arrived at Millie's in the middle of the night. They were clad only in their nightgowns, each of the girls clutching a bird cage, containing two budgerigars and two zebra finches respectively, birds that had been acquired by the children as pets, and which lived in the girls' bedroom. The scene resembled a wild parody of 'My old man said follow the van,' and was an event which was later recalled with laughter, but at the time, was part of a surreal nightmare for Anna. They were greeted by Millie, also in her nightdress, with her hair tangled and up on end, and her eyes popping, seeming to find the whole thing incredibly exciting and entertaining.

Anna found one of the worst aspects of her life at this time was the lack of a sense of security. She always felt that she was walking on a knife's edge, that at any moment some terrible quarrel would erupt, which could, and often did, result in violence. Granted usually things would subside, they would 'kiss and make up' and they could go several weeks in comparative peace. But, like living near an active volcano, she could never totally relax and she lived in constant fear for herself, but mainly for the children. She kept comforting herself by thinking, they will grow up eventually. They'll leave home. If only they get a good education, they will be alright. But, what should she do in the meantime, in the long years stretching interminably ahead, before they would become adults?

CHAPTER ELEVEN

In the mid nineteen eighties the Militant Tendency, or Militant, as it was referred to, came to power in the Liverpool City Council. Militant was a more left-wing and radical branch of the Labour Party, and their rise to power coincided with the increasingly desperate social and economic conditions in the city. Names like Tony Mulhearn, Peter Taaffe, Derek Hatton, Felicity Dowling and others were heard on everyone's lips.

Margaret Thatcher and her Tory government were trying to force savage financial cuts on the city's allowance for public expenditure, as they had all over the country. Known as the 'Liverpool 47', Militant's majority on the city council refused to implement the Tory cuts, using the slogan, 'Better to Break the Law than Break the Poor.' Eventually, because of Militant's determination to face up to the Tories, it came about that Liverpool's socialist-led council of 1983-87, was the only council in the country, which succeeded in extracting extra funding from

Taking Chances

Thatcher's government, because of its refusal to back down. Liverpool was a city prepared to fight, and it now had the chance to demonstrate its mettle.

The socialists or Militant, as they were popularly termed, came up with some new and revolutionary plans to improve conditions in the city. Housing was one of their priorities, and they set in train plans to demolish tenement and sub-standard housing, and implement a massive council house building scheme. Another of their areas of concern was education; they planned to establish seventeen Community Comprehensive Schools, following a massive re-organisation of education provision in the city, and it was in this area that Militant policy and the fate of Anna and Shola became entwined.

Shola had become more and more frustrated with his job at the financially struggling, and faction ridden, further education centre. He started to follow political events in the city closely, and he wisely decided that if he joined Militant, then perhaps he might be able to get a more secure teaching job in the state school system with their support. He started attending meetings, bringing some party members home, and generally getting politically and physically involved, although he drew the line at selling the newspaper, the 'Socialist Worker, on the streets . Anna enjoyed the visits, talking politics and meeting some new and stimulating acquaintances, some of whom later became friends. They were even invited to visit a key member of Militant at home in Liverpool, and they started to feel more connected with other people in the city. Anna was very glad to see Shola becoming more positive and hopeful about the future.

One evening he came home very exhilarated, tossing his briefcase down on the sofa, and exclaiming excitedly:

'They are going to create some jobs in race relations in the secondary schools. I think the title is Race Relations Co-ordinator or something like that. Apparently there will be some teaching, and the rest of the time will be spent in improving race relations in the school. It's long overdue as we all know how bad racism is in Liverpool. It took Militant to initiate this, but we, that is to say me, as well as some of the other black members, have advised them and now they seem to be listening. I'm getting the application forms tomorrow but I've been told that I have a good chance of getting one of these jobs.'

'That's wonderful'. Anna too was thrilled at the idea of some improvement in their circumstances, and she hoped that a new challenge might divert Shola's attention from the 'flaws' he perceived in the family, and that he might focus his attention and energies on a fresh and demanding job.

Shola and Anna slaved over the application form, submitted it promptly, and waited expectantly for a response. Sure enough, Shola was called for interview and offered a job on the same day. They celebrated by taking the whole family out for a Chinese meal. The restaurant was brightly decorated in Chinese style, with red and gold paper lanterns dangling from the ceiling, and boldly painted colourful pictures on the walls, depicting Chinese scenic landscapes. The children thoroughly enjoyed choosing their own meals from the menu, and being consulted and praised by the attentive waiter.

Shola was on a 'high' and in a very generous and expansive mood. After the meal, he lit a cigar, inhaled, and breathed out the pungent and heady aromatic smoke. For the first time in many months, he seemed to Anna like the upbeat, charismatic and happy man she had married. It was as if he had emerged from the dark clouds to find the proverbial silver lining. He made a fuss of the children, ensured they had ice cream and sweets after the meal, and was generally a different person from the morose moody man they knew. They were rather confused, but as children, they enjoyed the moment.

※

Shola started his new job a few weeks later. For the first six months he seemed happy, and totally consumed and energised by his new environment and responsibilities. He was full of the events of the day when he returned home from work each evening. Friends from Militant continued to figure in their lives, and sometimes they would visit them at home. Occasionally Shola, Anna and the children would travel to Liverpool to return visits or meet new people.

Anna continued her depressing job in Knowsley. She had by now, been placed in a few different schools, some better than others. In each she had eventually made the odd friend, which had rendered her days more bearable. Her friends were usually other supply teachers, people who for one reason or another were, like her, leading a nomadic existence moving from one school to another. Some were women who had taken time off work to have children, and who were finding it hard to get another permanent job, particularly during the current recession; others were men, quite often embittered by bad experiences within the system, possibly having been forced to leave their permanent post through ill health, failure to able to control their classes, clashes with a head teacher, or some real or rumoured misdemeanour.

One such, a middle aged Yorkshire man named Peter, had been her colleague at one of her placement schools, where he had been an established member of staff. Anna was very surprised to meet him again a year later, at another school in the borough, now reduced to her lowly level as a supply teacher. He explained to her that his headmaster had complained that he had trouble keeping his classes in order, and he had been asked to leave the school. The education authority had therefore decided to place him on the supply team. This man had been educated at Oxford, was a sound linguistics scholar, and a good kind man, but had not been tough enough to continue to survive the hurly burly of the classroom. Anna used to chat to him sometimes in the lunch hour, and enjoyed the commiserating companionship of a fellow sufferer. Peter subsequently developed severe depression, and eventually took early retirement on grounds of ill health.

Sometimes she managed to make some friends among the established teachers in a school. One year she was particularly friendly with a Danish woman, married to an Englishman, who was head of the home economics department at one of the schools where she was placed. They used to discuss a range of topics, such as school politics and rumoured scandals, disciplinary problems with their pupils, and their own children, over their sandwiches, and Anna actually felt human when she was with Anita. These friendships eased life, and her school experience, on a day to day basis, but it became very hard when she had to move on to a new placement and start all over again, usually after the end of each academic year.

※

One cold evening she was making her way home, passing through Liverpool city centre en route to the underground station. It was winter and it was almost dark. The shop windows radiated their bright warm lights, and the street decorations glittered and shone in the frosty air, giving the city streets an illusory fairytale charm. Anna stopped to look into the tinsel lined window of a book shop, thinking about what she might buy the children for Christmas. There was an enticing display of brightly coloured dustcovers on a wide range of children's books for all ages. Anna had always encouraged the children to read, and had read to them herself from when they were mere babies. The shop window looked like the entrance to an Aladdin's cave of promised delights. As she gazed intently and hopefully at the display, Anna became aware of another woman next to her, similarly occupied. She glanced to her side and then away, and then she looked again. Could it be? Could it possibly be Dorothy? Before the woman could move on again, Anna addressed her in a low voice.

'Dorothy?'

The other woman turned sharply and looked at her, and then she gasped.

Taking Chances

'Anna!'

They were both completely overcome with emotion. Tears trickled uncontrollably from Anna's eyes, blurring her vision, so she could hardly see her friend. Impulsively they hugged and then regarded each other searchingly. Anna could never know what Dorothy saw when she scrutinised her face, but she saw a new Dorothy, a confident and happy woman, not the wreck of a creature she had known in Jos.

'How long have you been in Liverpool?' Dorothy asked her, when they had both recovered from their excitement.

'About five years,' replied Anna. 'Whereabouts do you live? You must tell me everything and I will fill you in on what we have been doing.'

'We live in Allerton, that's Liverpool 15. Look, have you got twenty minutes, or so? We could go for a coffee.'

Even though Anna knew that she really should be getting home, there was no way that she could dream of refusing. They hurried to a nearby cafe, and sat down, their coffees in front of them. They could not get their words out quickly enough as they exchanged stories.

Dorothy told Anna that when she had first returned to her parents' house in the city back in 1980, she had been in a terrible state, both physically and psychologically. However, with their support, she had soon found a flat of her own, and started work as a classroom assistant. She had eventually gone on a part-time nursery teaching course, had qualified, and was now working as a full-time nursery teacher. She had also met a middle-aged Jamaican civil servant named Ray, and after she obtained a divorce from Jide, with many delays and great difficulty, she and Ray had got married. This had happened about two years previously.

Ray was a very good man, who was proving a wonderful father to her two children, and Dorothy was very much in love with him. Her children remained in touch with Jide and he had now accepted the situation, at first with resignation, but now with good grace. He had visited the family in Liverpool, and Dorothy and Ray had taken the children to visit him and his new wife in Jos the previous year. This had been a success and Dorothy felt that their relationship was now on a realistic and positive footing, and that they had put their troubled past well behind them.

She kept repeating her thanks to Anna for her help. 'Who knows what would have happened to us if you had not helped? I have never, and will never, forget what you did.'

'It was nothing. But I am so glad it all turned out so well. I wish my life could change direction too, but I am still optimistic that things will improve as the children get older.'

She gave Dorothy a rather watered down, and sanitized version of her own life at the moment, leaving out all the bad bits. She was aware that Dorothy was looking at her in a quizzical and concerned way, but brushed off any more searching questions that her friend tried to put to her.

Before parting, they exchanged addresses and telephone numbers, and vowed to keep in touch. They kissed and hugged again, and then each went her separate way.

Anna was confident that Dorothy would keep her promise and would contact her before long, but in her heart she knew it would be difficult to see her again because Shola would definitely oppose it. He would feel some solidarity with Jide, though, of course, he did not know anything about Anna's role in Dorothy's departure from Jos, and he could not know. But much more crucially, he was always very reluctant for Anna to make friends of her own.

Perhaps she would be able to see her friend secretly. At least she had her address and telephone number safely in her notebook, where it felt warm and reassuring in her pocket. For the first time in years Anna felt a glimmer of hope as she made her way hurriedly into the tube station. Once on the train, she sat down thankfully, in an unexpected and welcome vacant seat. The train soon entered the darkness of the tunnel, but while

Anna was busy thinking out excuses for her late arrival home, she retained something of the hope inspired by the Christmas lights.

CHAPTER TWELVE

Shola enjoyed having more money to spend as a result of his new job. Anna and he had agreed some years previously on their areas of financial responsibility: Shola would pay the children's school fees and half of the mortgage, while everything else fell to Anna. This meant that she paid for food for the family of five, utility bills, new clothes for herself and the children, as well as her own half of the mortgage. Particularly now, with his increased salary, it worked out that Shola always seemed to have spare cash for his own pleasures, including his cigarettes, drinks, and cannabis, and was still in a position to buy himself new and sometimes expensive clothes. Each month he enjoyed shopping for, and purchasing shirts, ties and the occasional suit, while still staying in credit at the bank.

On the other hand, Anna was always short of money, bought second-hand clothes for her and the children from charity shops, and the children's school uniform from second-hand sales at their schools, and was usually in the red. She dreaded the official letters, in their ominous brown envelopes, from her bank, summoning her for a humiliating interview with her bank manager, which left her feeling like a recalcitrant pupil hauled in front of the head master, to answer for her misdoings. Anna never complained to Shola about her financial state, because once again she felt the burden of guilt for their situation, and anyway it would have only resulted in an argument that she had no chance of winning.

Because Shola paid the school fees, he used the withdrawal of these payments as a threat whenever he was annoyed. This led to feelings of insecurity and fear in Anna, as she dreaded what the children might suffer in the state system, in the current climate of racism in their area. She was continually warning and exhorting the children to be careful not to annoy their father, so they were always walking on eggshells, and their resentment towards Shola grew in proportion to the atmosphere of threat.

As Shola suffered increasing disenchantment with his school job, he resumed the bullying and victimisation of the children. Femi largely escaped his father's attention; he was, of course, the youngest and a boy. The two girls, especially Shade, were constantly being shouted at, threatened and occasionally beaten. Shola expected that they should do all the housework in the home, in addition to their long days at school and their homework, and they had a rota for the washing up and other duties. Anna secretly used to do as much as she could to help them. However, she could never complain of feeling tired, as Shola would bellow:

'What are those two girls doing? At their age I was carrying pig fat on my head for my mother. You are spoiling them.'

The day after Anna's miraculous meeting with Dorothy, she felt a lightening of spirit. At last there would be someone to confide in, a true friend, who would properly understand her situation. Millie was a real comfort, but she could never fully appreciate Anna's experiences and preoccupations, or where she was coming from, in the way that Dorothy could.

As she did not want Shola to find out about Dorothy, and possibly forbid her from communicating with her again, Anna decided to phone her from a public telephone box on her way home from work, rather than risk her phoning the house. Dorothy was delighted to hear from her, and suggested that she come round for tea as soon as she could manage it. Anna remembered that she had a free lesson at the end of the day on the following Thursday, so she would say that she had a doctor's appointment and leave the school early. Thus it was arranged, and Anna looked forward eagerly to seeing Dorothy's home and meeting her family.

On the appointed day, Anna made her way by bus to Dorothy's house, which was situated in a pleasant residential suburb of Liverpool, Allerton, unusual for the city in the fact that it was quite racially mixed. It was slightly further out of the city centre than Toxteth, but was adjacent to it. Anna felt very excited by her illicit escape from her usual dreary routine, and she soon found Dorothy's house from the directions she had been given. The house stood in a terrace of similar brick built houses, but they were of good quality, with small gardens in front so that they were set well back from the road. Dorothy's own front garden was carefully tended with some pretty flowering shrubs, and a couple of stone urns full of brightly coloured flowers providing a focus of contrast from the dull red of the brickwork. Dorothy flung the front door open at her knock and embraced her warmly. She led her through to the back sitting room and introduced her to her husband, a friendly bear of a man: stout, slightly balding, with a beaming smile and kind eyes.

'Come on in and sit down. I've been really looking forward to meeting you,' he invited.

Ray had obviously been told all about Anna, and her role in helping Dorothy back in Jos; possibly he had also heard from Dorothy that she was now concerned about her friend, following their recent meeting. Dorothy's two children, Dipo and Bola, unrecognisable from the subdued and fretful youngsters she had seen in Jos, soon rushed into the room to be introduced to Aunty Anna. They looked happy and healthy, as they chattered away to their parents and Anna. Their complexions were so similar to those of Anna's children that her heart turned over and she felt sick; if only her three could also be as free to enjoy their childhood, and as happy as Dorothy's two. Anna could not help feeling envious of Dorothy and her new life with a loving and supportive partner.

Dorothy offered her tea and cake, which Anna accepted gratefully. It was so comforting to be sitting there, in a normal home, doing normal everyday things, like having a cup of tea, and chatting freely to friendly people, who wished her well. She wished the visit could go on and on, but it could only be fleeting, as she had to get home at the normal time to avoid any suspicion. Shola was very jealous, and he did not like her to have any outside friends whether he knew them or not. Perhaps he feared that if Anna confided in anyone she might start to question their relationship, and the status quo would be upset.

It was strange and almost unbelievable, that Anna felt herself to be powerless. Yet surely Shola did not feel himself as all powerful as Anna imagined. His tirades and outbursts of violence would have told any outsider that he felt extremely insecure himself. He had, however, managed to convince Anna that he was almost omnipotent, so that she had given up any hope of opposing him, or even discussing anything in a rational way, where there were differences of opinion, as useless and potentially dangerous.

When she had thanked Dorothy and Ray for their hospitality, she left, choking back tears, and promising to stay in touch, but warning Dorothy not to try to contact her at home. Even though Anna did not say much about Shola and her problems, what she did not say was as revealing as what she did, and her general depressed demeanour and emotional responses, told the true story to caring and perceptive friends.

'Make sure and let us know how you are. Remember we are here if you need us,' were Dorothy's parting words. Anna waved goodbye to the couple, who stood in the doorway, arms around the two children, all of them beaming at her.

As Anna travelled home by bus and train, she turned her situation over and over in her mind. Although she could not yet verbalise it to herself, somewhere deep down she was increasingly aware that her marriage was a failure. However, her pride would not let her admit this, even to herself. She and Shola had fought so hard to establish their relationship, despite the opposition of others, and perhaps even because of it, in the early days; her pride would not let her now admit that it had all been a mistake. She did not want their marriage to become yet another statistic on the roll call of the failure of mixed marriages. She could certainly not turn to her mother, who had been against them from the start. She would say that Anna had got herself into this situation, and would now have to live with her choice.

Another realisation was now dawning slowly on Anna: they should never have left Nigeria. Perhaps if they had stayed in Jos, Shola would not have become the embittered and angry man that he was now. He had been taken out of his familiar environment into a cold and hostile land, and this had exacerbated his paranoid and aggressive temperament. If they had stayed he might have been a professor by now, with the status that this post conferred, membership of the academic and social elite, instead of labouring as a lowly teacher in a Liverpool comprehensive. He would have had other outlets for his talents and would have felt less frustrated, so that then, perhaps, he would have been less hard on the children and her too.

The children, also, would have been better off. They would not be experiencing the racism and isolation that they currently faced, and would have been part of the privileged sector within their society, having friends who were either Nigerian or of similarly mixed backgrounds. Anna also was coming to understand that she did not belong here any more herself. She had nothing in common with the wider society in Britain any more than she had in Nigeria. Her marriage had put her 'beyond the pale'. She would never be fully accepted in the UK; even if she were not with Shola, the fact of being the mother of mixed race children would always set her apart. It had been a fallacy to imagine that by coming 'home' she would belong. Anna's loneliness and isolation overwhelmed her.

※

Over the next weeks and months, life continued much as before. There were numerous rows at home, Shola threatening and punishing the children, the atmosphere tense and heavy. If Anna and the children were home before Shola, they dreaded the sound of his key in the lock of the front door. Everyone felt themselves shudder as he entered the house; it was as if a heavy hand had descended on their pitiful attempts to be normal and happy, and was crushing them into the ground. Sometimes the rows escalated to the point of Anna making some half-hearted attempts to take the children and leave the house. However, because she always felt these attempts would be useless – Shola would definitely force them to come back – of course this was what happened in the end, and her pathetic rebellions always ended in defeat.

After such major rows, both Shola and Anna felt scared of what might have happened. At this time they still wanted, or imagined they wanted, their marriage to survive; Shola needed Anna, and Anna could not envisage life without him. There would be passionate reconciliations, and the air would clear for a few days before tension started to build again.

Looking back at this period, Anna later felt that she had been in a kind of trance; her sense of reality had become warped and she accepted her unnatural life as mandatory. She literally could not visualise any other option, even though she was vaguely aware that other people did not live in this way. She just had to get through it, and one day things would be better. The children would escape by going away to university. As yet, she could not even imagine what her own life with Shola would become, but at least the children would be safe.

Years would pass, wasted damaging years, with Anna in this deluded state. Largely due to her inertia, no single member of the family would survive without psychological scars that would mark them for life.

CHAPTER THIRTEEN

Three years later

The beatings had stopped. Perhaps Shola had somehow come to realise that he could not continue to get away with this form of abuse, now that the children were older, even though he claimed to consider it only normal parental discipline; perhaps he sensed that he might drive Anna over the edge, and that she might pluck up the courage to leave if he pushed things too far. He still threatened physical punishment, but for the past couple of years these fulminations had just been threats.

This did not mean that family life was now peaceful. That was far from being the case, as Shola was always picking on the children for one thing or another. There were continual conflicts, whether about their eating Nigerian food, about doing household chores, or about how the girls were dressed – Shola was always particularly critical of Lola in this regard.

'You're not going out in those kinds of clothes. Those shorts of yours are too tight. You look like a prostitute,' he would storm. 'Go up and change into something respectable!'

Lola would make a face, and go back upstairs. The three children whispered together about their hated father, and how they wished him dead, or anywhere but in the house with them. They had also grown to resent Anna for her weakness, and her refusal to stand up to their father's bullying ways.

He would not allow them to mix with local children. When they had first moved into the area, there had been some abortive attempts by a few neighbours to encourage their children to play together. Children had come knocking at their door, only to be turned away. Anna had tried in vain to change his mind on this, but Shola was adamant that he did not want his children mixing with the working class kids on the estate. This prohibition of course added to their isolation and their neighbours' dislike and distrust. Neither did he allow them to go to parties with their school friends, even though they were not working class. Just as he was jealous of Anna having outside friends, he seemed to resent the children for having any kind of social contact and tried his hardest to prevent it if he could.

The house seemed to shrink as the children grew bigger. Femi had the little box room, while the girls shared the largest bedroom, crammed full of their books, toys and clothes, as well as the bird cages, at the front of the house. Despite it being the most spacious bedroom, with their two beds, their various possessions, and the two bird cages, it was still claustrophobic. Shola and Anna had the second largest bedroom at the back, which was scarcely roomy enough to contain their double bed. They only had one small bathroom, and everyone competed to get into it at the same time. The overcrowding added to the strain in the family, as there was no personal space for anyone: if Shola was playing his music, the whole house shook and vibrated with the beat; if the children made any noise when the music was not on, they would be reprimanded, so they had to creep about to avoid getting called down and threatened with punishment.

Shola was more and more discontented with his job. He clashed frequently with the head teacher, a Mr Mason, who was very authoritarian and disliked being challenged in any way. As it was Shola's brief to act as advocate for the ethnic minority children in the school there were often conflicts. Sometimes a pupil might be excluded from school for some minor misdemeanour; at others a teacher might approach Shola for guidance on how to deal with the problems of a particular child. Shola also had to liaise with parents so that he often became a kind of buffer between the head teacher and the parents. It was an uneasy role. Added to this, Shola was the only black teacher in the school, and as such came under much closer scrutiny than the other teachers, especially in the racist climate of Liverpool. Any minor deviation from what was considered the norm could put him in trouble. Having to be so careful to avoid confrontation, not always successfully, added to his already high stress levels and his frustration with life in general.

Shade had spent the past two years attending a local grammar school. After her O levels she had transferred there from her private school in Liverpool to save the cost of fees; it was also better for her as Shola had not been able to threaten to withdraw funds for her fees. Despite the years of bullying, her spirit was undaunted, and she had great aspirations for her future. Now she was awaiting the results of her Advanced level exams, and as such had acquired slightly more status in Shola's eyes. She planned to go to university if she got the requisite grades, and her desire to escape home had motivated her to work very hard in preparation for the exams, as well her natural ambition to do well. Lola, on the other hand, now continually clashed with her father.

Lola had always been Shola's favourite. Back in the days of Jos, it had been she who had helped him with his birds and followed him around the yard. While Shade had avoided contact as much as possible, Lola had a reasonably good relationship with Shola for much of her life. Now, however, Lola challenged her father where the others, and that included Anna, did not dare. She was fifteen years old, and resented very bitterly the fact that she was not allowed to go to parties and clubs like her classmates. This did not worry Shade so much, as encouraged by Anna, she was biding her time in the hope that university would bring her some much desired, but so far denied, social life. Shade had suffered too much from her father's temper to challenge him. In fact, on numerous occasions Lola had argued with him on Shade's behalf, earning them both further punishments.

Anna became increasingly concerned about Lola. She herself had never been close to her second daughter and felt guilty about this. She had been so preoccupied with trying, usually in vain, to shield Shade from her father's bullying and to comfort her, that Lola had been completely neglected emotionally. Anna hoped that when Shade departed for university she would be able to attempt to repair this damage, but she did not know then that it had been left too late.

Lola had just completed her GCSE's; she was in the first batch of pupils to take these exams. It was the summer holidays, the weather was hot, and the children were bored with being cooped up in the stuffy house, like animals in cages at the zoo. Lola used to sit brooding on her bed, in the room she shared with Shade. She was often rude and abusive with Anna:

'Don't touch me. You revolt me!' she would say when Anna tried to hug her, much to Anna's discomfiture and distress.

When Femi attempted to go into the girls' room at Shade's invitation, Lola would either throw things at him or lunge at him. The little boy had to run the gauntlet of passing by Lola's bed, in his effort to reach the safety of Shade's side of the room.

A major row erupted one afternoon as Lola refused to come out of the bathroom, when Shola wanted to go to the toilet. He ended up having to go to the local pub to use the toilet, and was, of course, incandescent with fury, uttering threats and imprecations against his daughter. Anna became increasingly fearful that Lola might be in physical danger from her father if she continued to defy him.

As if all the conflicts in the family were not enough, they started to endure racial abuse and harassment from a new family, who had recently moved into the next door house. On one occasion, there was a large party of people in the next door garden, ostensibly having a barbeque, but clearly having been invited there to intimidate their neighbours. Anna's family were subjected to mocking and jeering from these people, set up to it by their hosts.

'Nigger, go back to your own country!' someone shouted, to the cheers and hoots of the others.

'Fucking wogs,' another added, to more mocking laughter.'

Anna could not believe what she was hearing; it seemed like a bad dream. As the shouts from next door became ever more menacing, they all started to feel really frightened, even Shola, though he put up a bold front. It was as if these people were a lynch mob baying for their blood, even though this was Merseyside in the nineteen eighties, not Alabama in the thirties. The situation got so bad that Shola had to phone the police, despite the fact that he hated to have anything to do with them.

'Are you quite sure that you heard the word "nigger"?' queried one of the officers, in a doubtful and unbelieving tone, when they finally arrived on the scene.

Their neighbours were cautioned, but civil relations were now impossible. They could no longer go out into the garden without fear of an unpleasant encounter. Shola's gardening, one of his few solaces, now became problematical, and might even trigger a new confrontation across the low fence which divided their property from that of their neighbours.

Anna decided that they would have to move, not only because of the racism they were experiencing, but also because they desperately needed more space. Her family members had become like rats in a small trap, and as such, were turning on one another with ever increasing ferocity. Anna, with her usual grim optimism, believed that if they had a larger house they might avoid some of the conflicts that were now threatening to explode into violence.

She discussed the situation with Shola and they decided to put their house on the market. Shola was not as keen about the idea of moving as Anna, as he hated any kind of change. However, this time Anna was determined. She consulted an estate agent, a 'for sale' sign was erected in the front garden, and Anna quietly started going to look at houses in better areas.

At about this time, Shola heard about an anti-racist support group that had been set up on the Wirral. He got in touch with the organisers and it was agreed that he and Anna would attend their next group meeting. Anna was pleased that at least they would have some people to turn to when the situation with the neighbours escalated again.

Anna and Shola turned up to the meeting, which was being held in a local primary school. They travelled there by bus as the meeting place was situated in another part of the Wirral, a few miles away from where they lived. The group members ranged quite widely in age but, on looking around, Anna noticed that they were all white and middle class. Shola and Anna were eyed with curiosity by the group, as if they were a form of rare and exotic animal, but when they told their story of the harassment they were experiencing, they were assured that they would no longer be alone. In future, if any untoward events occurred they could phone some members of the group who would come to their house and show solidarity with them. It was hoped that this would deter their neighbours from any further overt acts of racism.

After the meeting was over, Anna and Shola were approached by a very slim middle aged woman wearing jeans and a striped top. She had long blonde hair, a beaky nose and very intense pale blue eyes.

'Hello. I'm Rachel Martin. I've got five children, three white and two mixed race. It would be lovely if you could come over to our house next Sunday. We are having a small party for some of our friends and their children. We can come and pick you up if you don't have transport. And, of course, bring your children.'

'That would be lovely,' both Anna and Shola agreed.

A time was set and then they made their way home, feeling, for the first time in ages, a degree of hope, and also a relief from their terrible isolation.

Shade and Femi were excited at the idea of going to a party; Lola was grumpy and negative, but she did not really have an option. They started to plan what they would wear from their limited charity shop wardrobe, and even Anna could not help being hopeful that at last they might, as a family, start to make friends on the Wirral.

CHAPTER FOURTEEN

Sunday arrived, and the Martins drew up opposite their house in a large white Volkswagon people carrier. Anna could imagine that the neighbours were agog as her family very seldom had visitors. Net curtains twitched, as Shola, Anna and the children walked down the path in their best clothes, the children's faces, particularly those of Shade and Femi, reflecting their excitement at the novelty of the occasion, and were greeted effusively with hugs and kisses by the Martins, before climbing into the car.

The Martins' house was in a leafy residential suburb, and was large and detached with an extensive garden. Rachel's husband was also blond and blue- eyed; he was of a similar age to his wife and very friendly and affable. Anna and Shola were amazed to see a large number of people in the Martins' lounge. But the most interesting and unusual thing they noticed immediately, was that all the adults were white, and all the children seemed to be of mixed race. This was not strictly true, as the Martins had three blond blue-eyed children of their own, but they also had two mixed race adopted daughters.

'Come and meet our friends,' Rachel invited them, smiling warmly, and indicating chairs for them to sit down.

The other couples all seemed be accompanied by at least one or two children of mixed race. Most of the adults appeared to be in their forties, were casually dressed, several of the men sporting long hair and beards. They all looked ecstatic to see Shola and Anna, with their children; perhaps they represented what had long dwelt in their imaginations, and they could see now in real life, the reality of the kind of union which had produced their own foster and adopted children.

Anna could not help but be fascinated, but at the same time slightly disturbed, to see all these comfortable white people, who probably had little or no idea of what it must be like to be black in a racist society, responsible for the welfare of these vulnerable children, who would have to face that racism individually, as they grew up and went to school in all white areas. She wondered how they could possibly create and nurture in their children a feeling of pride in their black identity, with no adult black role model in their families.

Then she felt ashamed. What right had she to judge? What kind of role model did her own children have? A father who was either bullying them unmercifully or was flat out in a cannabis-induced stupor; did that constitute a positive role model? Moreover, he ironically produced the opposite effect than he intended when he talked about African culture. Ostensibly he wished to inculcate in them pride and positivity in their African roots, yet he seemed to delight in the punitive and deprived aspects of the culture, rather than the positive achievements of African people in music, the arts and scholarship. No wonder her children were growing up with negative feelings about their black heritage. Perhaps these well meaning white people might be able to help their adopted children to admire the achievements of black people, having made a conscious decision to adopt black youngsters, and having a desire to see the best in the race from which these children derived at least half of their identity.

Rachel introduced Anna and Shola to the other adults at the party. She also took a great interest in Shade and Lola, though less, for some reason, in Femi. She encouraged the girls to make friends with her own daughters, and to visit them again as soon as it could be arranged. Lola was unforthcoming, still grumpy and resentful about being forced to come on this visit, but Shade seemed quite keen to develop the relationship. Rachel also mentioned that she and her family would be going on a week's camping holiday in Wales very shortly, and she urged Anna's children to join them. Anna said that they would consider the idea and thanked Rachel very profusely for her generous offer.

The party continued with a buffet meal, after which the children gathered in front of the television to watch a video of 'The Color Purple', based on Alice Walker's novel of the same name, which they all seemed to find spell-binding. Later there was a sing-song; one of the fathers produced a guitar and everyone joined in singing popular camp fire songs. Shola and Anna were slightly embarrassed by all this, as it was not really their sort of thing, but they were generally pleased by the day, and felt quite positive when they returned home.

'I think it would be a really good idea to take Rachel up on her offer about the holiday. It would do the children good to get away. It's awfully cramped and hot in this house at the moment', Anna suggested tentatively, later that evening. She did not really expect that Shola would agree.

Surprisingly he also thought it would be a good idea. The only person who was not enthusiastic was Lola, when the plan was put to the children the following morning.

'I don't want to go,' she asserted.

'Please say yes, Lola. It will be a lovely break for you. You'll have fun. It won't be very nice for you here on your own if the others are away.'

After considerable persuasion, by both Anna and the other two children, Lola eventually agreed to go. How Anna wished later that she had not put so much pressure on her, but she genuinely thought that a holiday, away from the hot claustrophobic house and an irritable father, was what all the children needed. Also she herself badly needed a break from acting as a buffer between them all during the unremitting conflicts of the past weeks.

The children were away for a week. Anna waved them off with mixed feelings. On one hand she would worry about them, as they had rarely spent a night away from home, but she was also very glad that they would have some carefree time in a child friendly environment.

Strangely, Anna and Shola themselves had a very peaceful week, the first they had enjoyed without the children since Shade's birth eighteen years previously. It was almost like a honeymoon. They had never had a real one, but now they went over to Liverpool, ate out and revelled in some quiet evenings in, with just the two of them. Shola was a different person when he was alone with Anna, charming and good company. It seemed that he really did just want her to himself, and was quite unable to integrate the children into the relationship, or to communicate with them in any meaningful way. Their being around was an irritant, and distraction for Shola, from what was most important to him, Anna and himself, and their marriage. This peaceful week was to be the calm before the storm.

When the children got back from their holiday, Anna was quick to notice a change in Lola. After all the weeks of sitting dull eyed and broody on her bed, she was suddenly sparkling and excited. She talked a lot about the holiday, and especially about one of Rachel's sons, Jacob, who she really liked. Shade and Femi were more muted in their appreciation of the trip, though they had enjoyed it, but Lola could not stop reliving every minute of it.

※

Exam results loomed. Anna accompanied Shade to her school to get her Advanced Level results on the second Thursday in August. Shade was very nervous; such a lot depended on her getting the grades to go to university, not least the chance to leave home. She had even fortified herself with a couple of glasses of sherry, given to her surreptitiously by Anna, before leaving home, so that she could face the morning, and what it might bring.

'Mummy, do you think I will get my grades?' Shade agonised.

'Of course you will,' Anna assured her, though she worried inwardly.

At the school, all the girls waiting for their results were in a state of stress and tension, as they sat on seats set out in the corridor outside the head's office, some on their own and others with anxious parents. They had to go into the headmistress's office one by one to receive their grades, and they waited both nervously and impatiently, for their name to be called.

Anna was tense herself, though she kept trying to calm and reassure Shade, hoping fervently that the results would be good. Fortunately, Shade found to her joy and relief that she had passed all her subjects, not quite highly enough to get into her first choice of university, but well enough to be accepted at her second. The whole family were genuinely ecstatic, with the exception of Lola who scowled her discontent. She dreaded Shade leaving home, as she feared that she would then become the full focus for Shola's negative attention.

They went out for a meal at their favourite Chinese restaurant to celebrate Shade's success; Shola even promised to fund Shade's purchase of a pair of contact lenses and some new

Taking Chances

clothes before she started at university. She would be attending Lancaster University and studying social sciences.

Both the other two children were also changing schools that September. Lola was due to enrol at the local sixth form college, and Femi was to start at minor public school for boys. This would mean that Shola would only have one set of fees to pay, in addition to Shade's maintenance at the university. Everything seemed on course to change for the better. They had even received an offer on their house, and had found a large Victorian semi-detached, much nearer to the town, for a very good price.

Anna was just daring to feel that perhaps at last there was the proverbial light at the end of the tunnel, when her carefully constructed fool's paradise collapsed around her ears.

The week following Shade's exam results, Anna went to Liverpool with Lola to collect her GCSE grades from her school. Unfortunately, Lola had passed only five out of her eight subjects. Of course she had not studied properly; she had preferred to watch a pop concert rather than revise on the night before an important exam, and her heart had not been in her studies anyway. She was, moreover, living through the most difficult years in her young life, in a highly dysfunctional family. Now she was angry and defiant:

'They must have made a mistake. I'm going to ask for a re-mark,' she shouted, with tears of frustration streaming down her cheeks.

'Don't worry,' comforted Anna. 'I'm sure you have enough passes to go to the college, and you can always re-sit the subjects you failed.'

From that day on, Lola was beyond Anna's reach. She was not used to performing less well than her sister. She was also going through a stormy adolescence in very difficult conditions, and no leeway was given in their house for teenage angst. She became increasingly erratic in her behaviour: one minute she was sullen and withdrawn, the next abusive and violent. She hit out at Femi and Shade, and once at Anna herself. Anna dared not let Shola know what was going on; she had learned not to involve him in any disciplinary issues, as his reprisals would far outweigh the offence.

Anna kept hoping nevertheless that somehow things would hold together until they moved into their new house and Shade went to university. However, this was not to be.

※

She could never remember exactly how the row developed. It filled the sky like a sudden summer storm with little warning. Possibly she had blocked out the details, as one blocks out things that are too painful to remember. All she could recall was Shola shouting, the children retreating to their rooms, and then shortly afterwards, the three of them coming down the stairs together, and going into the kitchen. Unknown to her, they did not stop there. They left the house by the back door and did not return.

When it became obvious that they were not in the kitchen, but had actually left the house, Shola and Anna phoned around among their acquaintances, and discovered to their relief that all three children were safe, and were with Rachel Martin. Apparently they had gone first to Millie's and then by taxi to the Martins' house.

Perhaps subconsciously it was almost a relief for Anna, rather like the feeling after a painful boil had been lanced. Now other people would be involved; maybe someone would be able to help them achieve some sort of equilibrium in their family. Surely Shola would have to learn to control his temper. She had been afraid for Lola for some time, as she too, did not know where to stop in aggravating her father.

Unfortunately, in these situations, it is never that simple, not least since they had been informed that Social Services had been called in. Anna had begged Rachel to delay doing this, hoping that even at this point some informal solution would be found, which would give them a breathing space to sort things

Taking Chances

out. Rachel was however adamant that she must inform the authorities. Of course, she was a council foster parent and had a good relationship with Social Services. Anna realised then, as if a tidal wave had engulfed her, taking away any chance of autonomous action, that things were out of their hands, and she knew the real meaning of paralysing fear. Was her weakness about to exact from her the most terrible penalty? Was she going to lose her children?

CHAPTER FIFTEEN

The next few days took on a nightmare quality. Shola and Anna were summoned to the Social Services offices. Shade and Lola were already there.

Social Services were housed in a nondescript grey building in a side street in downtown Birkenhead. The building itself looked grimy and down at heel, reflecting the human failures and hardship that it witnessed daily. The waiting room contained dismal brown chairs with ripped seat covers, and torn magazines, tossed around in a higgledy piggledy fashion, littered a small central table. The place smelt of poverty and fear, a stale sharp stench, which might fill even the most stout-hearted client with despair and foreboding.

They were eventually shown into a small dingy office, with dirty, finger print smeared windows, and a smell of stale cigarette smoke. Used coffee mugs, and the circles they had created on desks and papers, adorned the visible surfaces, amid piles of paperwork and files. Shade and Lola were sitting on straight backed chairs facing two female social workers; Anna and Shola were nodded towards two similar chairs some distance from the girls.

The two women seemed to be both in their late thirties. The senior of the two was obviously middle class, from her accent and general demeanour, and was named Jane Thomas. She was slim with light brown hair to her shoulders, and her rather tired face wore a cool determinedly neutral expression. She was casually dressed in a cream coloured sweater and tweed skirt. She adopted the stance of a concerned and reasonable professional, and spoke to Anna and Shola in a courteous and calm manner. Her more junior colleague, Rita Jones, with her dark hair fastened in a ponytail, and face caked in thick make-up, was a hard faced Scouser, a marked contrast in every way to Miss Thomas, and seemed to dislike Anna on sight, taking no trouble to hide her feelings.

Anna could not help feeling that these two female social workers, particularly Rita, judged her as the most culpable party in the whole sorry affair, and took an almost punitive delight in her distress; they were both obviously judging her for her relationship with a black man, and her middle class accent seemed to antagonise them even more than if she had been working class. She was shocked to see the senior social worker offer both her daughters cigarettes. How could they do such a thing to young girls who had never smoked before in their lives?

The junior social worker, speaking in her broad Scouse accent, adopted an almost hectoring tone whenever she addressed Anna. She seemed to blame her solely for the situation. Obviously she had jeopardised her children's happiness in order stay with a wretched man, who she should never have married in the first place; this was the message she was receiving subliminally from both the two women. As they sat in the dilapidated and depressing office, Anna felt that she had reached the depths of humiliation and defeat.

The two girls were questioned by Jane Thomas about what they wanted to do. Lola was determined that she wanted to stay with Rachel Martin. As the latter was a licensed foster parent, it could apparently be easily arranged that Lola could live with the Martins, and this option seemed to have been discussed before the meeting by Rachel and the social workers. Rachel was in fact a foster parent for Liverpool, but the Social Services could get round this to enable her to foster for Wirral also. Anna begged Lola to change her mind, but the thought of escaping her father, particularly now that Shade was about to leave for university, and the attraction of living with the Martins, and especially their children, outweighed any arguments that Anna could muster. And besides, Lola was now full of resentment towards her mother.

Shade, on the other hand, instinctively distrusted the social workers. In any case, she was soon to go to university and she felt she had more to lose by leaving home at this point, as she was dependent on her father paying her maintenance. She tried to dissuade her sister from putting herself in care but to no avail. Both girls were in agreement on one point: Femi would come to no harm if he returned to his parents. For these assertions by her daughters, Anna was eternally grateful.

Anna and Shola were presented with two equally unpleasant choices: they could either sign papers putting Lola into 'voluntary care', or if they refused, Social Services would apply to the court to have her put in compulsory care. Jane Thomas, the more sympathetic of the two social workers, advised the former option, as she said that they would have more chance of their daughter returning to them if they put her into what they termed 'voluntary care,' a misleading euphemism in their particular case.

Eventually Shola and Anna were virtually forced to sign the papers. Anna did insist, however, on inserting a sentence to say that they were only signing because they were under duress. As they left the social services office, a triumphant Rita could not resist hissing vindictively at Anna,

'You'll never get your daughter back now....'

Back at home, Shola and Anna faced each other with their now diminished family. Everyone was too shocked for further conflict. Anna hugged Femi to her, relief at getting him back to some small extent comforting her for the loss of Lola. Anyway, she was determined that Lola would return before too long.

※

The next couple of weeks were filled with preparing for Shade to go to university: buying her some new clothes, including a pretty party dress, really new, and not from a charity shop; getting her fitted with contact lenses; and purchasing a brand new trunk in which to pack all her belongings. When the day arrived, Shola, Anna and Femi accompanied her on the train to Lancaster, thrilled and yet filled with trepidation, not quite knowing what to expect, all of them with their own hopes and fears. They soon found themselves in her sparsely furnished, but clean and bright room at her chosen hall of residence, with its single bed, bookshelves waiting to be filled, and a new desk and chair facing the window.

The hall was bustling with new students and their parents, excited and elated at the novelty of their shared enterprise. Most of the students could not wait to plunge into university life, while their parents, like adult birds whose fledglings were at last learning to fly, felt a sense of achievement themselves, that their offspring had reached this important turning point in their individual lives. Some of the mothers' excitement was tempered a little, by the thought of their impending parting with their son or daughter, and worry about their welfare in this strange environment; the fathers seemed almost without exception, confident in their children, and full of reassurances to their doubtful spouses.

Shola and Anna were bursting with pride, and Anna hoped desperately that Shade would settle quickly in to university life, and that she would have some long overdue happiness, now that she was independent of her difficult home circumstances. It was hard to leave her though, and both Anna and Shade wept on saying goodbye; Femi too shed a tear at leaving his sister behind, and having to return home without her.

※

Shola was very subdued following the departure of both his daughters. However, he seemed to burst back into life, when they were contacted by Social Services with the proposition that they should meet with Lola, in order to discuss the issues that had led to her going into care.

The meeting was predictably unsuccessful, as there was too much emotion on both sides. The outcome was that Lola said she was willing to meet again with Anna, but not her father. Anna would have been glad to have the opportunity to talk to Lola, to try to persuade her to return home, but Shola would not hear of this arrangement.

'If you do that, she will never come back home. No, if you do not agree, she will be forced to change her mind. Anyway, I am forbidding you to see her without me. She will either see us both or neither of us.'

Anna understood regretfully that there would be no point in arguing. She thought that perhaps if she left it for a few weeks she would find some way of communicating with her daughter.

※

She had been in touch with Dorothy on and off over the past few years, seeing her a few times when she had been able to steal an hour on her way back from work, either to visit Dorothy at her house, or meet up with her in the city centre. Now she telephoned her friend:

'Dorothy, what shall I do? I must get Lola back. Shola is impossible – I just can't talk to him. All he says is that we must use a lawyer to contest the care order. But even if we won, we can't force Lola to come home. I'm desperate.'

'I really feel for you, Anna. Perhaps you should give it a few months and see how things develop. It may be better for Lola to be out of the house for a while – at least you won't have to worry about something violent happening. It will give both Shola and Lola time to cool off. Don't blame yourself. You have done everything you could.'

'But should I leave Shola? In some ways I feel I would, if it would make any difference to my relationship with Lola. But right now I feel that she is so angry that we would not be able to live together anyway. I'm also thinking of Femi. He's only just started at his new school, and I certainly can't afford to pay his fees at such an expensive place. I would hate to deny him the chance of a first class education, as I am so unsure about where I stand with Lola. She seems to hate me, not that I blame her for that. Also because she has been violent towards the other children and me, I'm not really sure I can control her. We might just be back to square one, even if she were to live with me and Femi.'

'I think that you should give it some time, and see how things go. Are you still moving to your new house?'

'Yes, next week. I'm making sure that we keep a room for Lola for when she comes back.'

Anna still deluded herself that somehow everything would be resolved, sooner rather than later, and the move was part of her plan. Dorothy reminded her to keep her informed of progress, and they agreed to see each other after Anna had moved to her new house.

CHAPTER SIXTEEN

Anna was very optimistic and excited about their new home. Even though it was in a rather decayed area, the house itself was in good condition. It had four levels, including a large basement containing the kitchen, which was big enough to contain a dining table, and crucially an additional shower room and toilet. At least there would be no more wrangles about access to the bathroom.

The house was carpeted from top to bottom. Everything seemed magical and full of promise to Anna as they looked around, so that she felt like Alice discovering Wonderland. All the rooms were large with high decorated ceilings, and the two ground floor living rooms both contained ornate Victorian stone fireplaces, one with patterned and colourful tiles. Even the hallway was huge, and the upstairs staircase led to two floors of bedrooms, so that each of the children could have their own study/ bedroom. Femi was to have an attic room on the top floor, with a sloping roof and masses of space for all his things, including the two bird cages with their noisy and cheerful occupants, which were now his responsibility. Anna planned that Lola would have the room next to his, if and when she returned home.

Shade's room would be next to that of Shola and Anna, on the first floor; this floor also had a very large bathroom, with a huge pink oval shaped bath and toilet fittings. It was luxury compared to their previous cramped conditions, and it would also mean that there would be less chance of conflict, as family members could keep their distance from each other if they wanted to, because there was so much space.

Shola had once again subsided into depression following the abortive attempt at meeting with Lola. Anna realised that she would have to do most of the work for the move, and accordingly, she organised all the packing, and directed the removal men on the location of packing cases and furniture. Moving day was exhausting, but was over eventually. Shola appeared totally disorientated. He huddled, wrapped in a blanket, in front of the television in the new house. He seemed unsure of where he actually was, and seemed to be totally in his own world. Little did Anna know it at the time, but this was to be the pattern of the next few months.

Shola aroused himself from his lethargy and despair only when he felt that they might be able to do something to bring Lola back home. Accordingly, he insisted that they use the services of a solicitor to contest Lola's placement in care. Anna soon found herself with Shola, visiting the office of a female lawyer over in Liverpool. She had no faith in the legal process producing any positive results, but Shola clung desperately to the idea that there had been a miscarriage of justice, which could and should be rectified. Anna knew deep down that if Lola did not wish to return home, and goodness knew she had enough grounds to find the idea repulsive, no court would force her to do so. But she had to play along with the charade, and it helped Shola to have some hope, that his deep psychic pain would be eased, and of course, that he would be proved to be in the right.

The lawyer's office was located at the top of an old eighteenth century building, situated near the High Court, and other legal institutions. They had chosen their particular lawyer, whose name they had picked out from the Yellow Pages, purely because she claimed to be experienced in family law and they hoped that she would be sympathetic to their situation.

Anna and Shola entered the specified building, and checked to find out if they were in the right place, by scanning the brass plates displayed in the lobby. They identified their lawyer's name, and discovered, to Anna's dismay, that her office was on the top floor of the high, narrow house. They were therefore forced to enter the miniscule lift, looking like an airtight metal box, which Anna eyed with dread, as she hated the claustrophobia these tiny lifts produced in her, and soon found themselves outside the office of their legal adviser.

Miss Rupert turned out to be an elderly wizened figure, of indeterminate age, with dyed hair, of indeterminate colour, but with very determined opinions. She barely listened to their story, even though Anna kept trying to correct some of her misconceptions, but was soon offering to write letters on their behalf to various authorities, surmising rather than ascertaining the actual facts of the case. Anna was in despair at the potential waste of time and money generated by their involvement with Miss Rupert, but Shola was hopeful of some positive outcome. Even he was daunted a few weeks later, however, when their letters proved fruitless, just as Anna had secretly always known they would be, and they were presented with a huge bill, far in excess of any reasonable recompense for services rendered, and they were forced to take on a new battle by refusing to pay the exorbitant sum demanded. They did refer the matter to the Law Society who eventually adjudicated that they were in the right, and the bill was adjusted downwards accordingly. All of this had not helped in retrieving Lola, and as Anna had feared, had actually been a total waste of time and effort.

Apart from when they visited Miss Rupert to discuss Lola's case, or when they jointly composed letters to Social Services of their own, they hardly communicated. Shola continued to go to work, but all his time in the new house was spent in watching television, or soft porn videos. He would then smoke cannabis, lighting up spliffs, one after the other, until he fell asleep. He seemed to be deteriorating mentally and physically; he still looked smart when he went to work, but at the weekends he became a wreck. He did not bath or shave, and he sometimes did not even dress.

Anna was in despair, but she did realise and understand that Shola was going through a deep depression, following the departure of Lola. His whole world picture had been shattered, especially his ideas, or illusions, about the family, and what he expected a family to be. He was unwilling or unable to discuss his feelings, so she must just wait it out and hope that he would come through and back to his normal, or at least properly functioning, self. She was consumed with guilt now, not just about Lola, but also about Shola. She tried to be cheerful herself for Femi's sake, but her loneliness, regret, and often desperation about how their lives had turned out, sometimes overwhelmed her.

Anna had always believed in God. She had gone through a very religious phase in her teens, had attended church on a fairly regular basis even whilst at university, and though in recent years she had only been to church very occasionally, she had always felt deep down, that there was a Higher Being who cared about her. Indeed, it was this belief that had sustained her through the most difficult periods of her life; attending church on and off for most of her life, even if sporadically, had helped her to feel a degree of comfort. An unfortunate experience, the last time she had gone to church, however, had put her off making the effort to actually attend a service, or to be part of any organised religion. Feeling cast adrift from any contact with the church had only added to her loneliness, and sense of alienation.

It had been on a Christmas Eve, a couple of years previously, and Anna, yearning to recapture the religious sense and meaning of Christmas, remembered from her childhood, had decided to attend the Midnight Mass at her local Anglican church. Shola had not been keen to accompany her, and none of the children showed any interest in religion, so she wrapped up against the winter cold, and made her way to the church, which was situated about ten minutes walk from the house

The church was packed. Anna found a pew towards the front, and slipped quietly into her place. Later, during the service, she became conscious of a peculiar noise coming from somewhere behind her. It seemed that a member of the congregation, obviously worse for the wear from pre-Christmas over drinking, was retching and vomiting, emitting both a disgusting sound and a revolting stench.

The offending individual was bundled out of the church, and the service proceeded. However, when the minister rose to give his sermon, he was obviously very annoyed and upset by what had just happened. Though he did his best not to appear in any way affected, he gave a grave homily, soundly condemning those people who only attended church on occasions like Christmas. Anna felt very guilty, and also unwelcome, almost a pariah, on hearing this sermon, and had not returned to that church, or any other, since.

She still prayed nightly, but now she did feel that God had abandoned her, or that perhaps she was not worth His love or compassion. All she felt was hopelessness. She was going through the motions of a normal life, but inside a small voice kept repeating, 'What is the point of it all?' intruding into her consciousness with cruel regularity, like a niggling toothache, and she had no answer to the insistent and painful question.

CHAPTER SEVENTEEN

Shola gradually came out of his depression, as the months passed since Lola's departure from the family. He began to grow accustomed to their new house, and he enjoyed getting the garden into shape, even having a brand new greenhouse installed. He would spend hours in the garden, especially in the greenhouse, where he would pot and re-pot his vegetable plants, water them all lovingly, and take a tremendous pride in his produce. It seemed to be a therapeutic outlet, where he could forget the stresses of work and the disappointments of home life. He very seldom shouted in the house these days, now that the girls had both gone, and he left Femi alone.

Anna and he were united on one issue at least, as they were both determined that Lola should continue in full time education, despite being in foster care. They put pressure on Social Services in the form of their lawyer's letters, as well as those written by them personally, insisting that Lola came from a family that set great store by education, and that they would be willing to go to court to ensure that she continued with her studies, and went to college. In this, at least, they were successful, and Lola enrolled at the sixth form college to do her Advanced levels.

One day, some months later, they received a telephone call from Social Services, asking them to come in to their office. The social worker who telephoned was unwilling to disclose the reason for the call, but just said that they should come in as soon as possible. When they arrived at the now familiar building, full of its bad memories, both very anxious, fearing that something bad had happened to Lola, the visibly embarrassed social workers had to confess to Anna and Shola, that Lola had been arrested for shoplifting in the town centre of Birkenhead. Apparently, she had got into bad company and this was the result. It now appeared that Rachel Martin was not Super Mum, despite her fostering credentials, and her 'experience', with mixed race children.

Anna felt very bitter towards Rachel, blaming her, possibly unjustly, for Lola's defection. In Anna's eyes, Rachel had managed to get hold of one of her daughters, something Anna felt instinctively that she had wanted, almost single-mindedly, as soon as she had met the family. Unfortunately, they had played into her hands. However, Anna ruefully reflected, children were not just dolls to be added to a collection, and Rachel was not proving any more competent than Anna herself, in bringing up her troubled teenager. Fortunately, as Lola had never been in trouble before, she had been let off by the police with a caution.

Femi too was growing up, becoming a handsome and talented young man, and Anna doted on him; she was unable to express this openly for fear of Shola's jealousy. He was a very responsible boy and a 'latch-key kid', in that he arrived home from school well before Anna and Shola got back from Liverpool. He would wash up the breakfast dishes, make his own tea, and have started his homework, by the time his parents got home. He was very

Taking Chances

gifted academically, consistently scoring top grades, and also a promising actor, performing to great acclaim in school productions. Filled with pride, Shola and Anna, dressed in their best clothes, would listen to his masters extolling his talents when they attended Parents' Evenings at his school.

These Parents' Evenings were held regularly, events where the masters, august in their academic gowns, would sit at desks in the impressive school hall, lined with portraits of past head masters, facing queues of anxious parents. The parents, all smartly dressed for the occasion, would chat to each other while waiting for the masters to be free to talk to them, and would sometimes be offered refreshments, so it became something of a social affair. All the masters would give glowing reports of Femi's progress, and prophesy great things for his future: 'He will definitely get in to Oxford or Cambridge,' was the common refrain.

Other parents would occasionally congratulate them also, as they heard from their own sons about Femi's achievements. As Shola and Anna walked home after these events, they felt proud and optimistic; surely they must be doing something right to have such a promising son.

It gradually became clear that Lola would not be returning home. Anna felt as if she had had a limb amputated, but like a physical cripple, she adjusted to the loss, though was never able to forget it. From the time that Lola had gone into care, Anna felt herself a criminal. Even when she was not conscious of thinking about her lost child, she always had a numb sensation at the back of her head, reminding her that there was something wrong in her life: it would never be perfect, or even good, again.

She had some limited contact with Lola sporadically, but always in secret. They would occasionally arrange to meet up in Birkenhead, but these meetings were inevitably and invariably, unsatisfactory and painful, with Lola accusatory and Anna defensive. Eventually they stopped trying.

While all these traumas had been going on in her home life, Anna had continued to teach on the supply team in Knowsley. She never knew how she managed to go into school every day, but she did. She was too ashamed to confide in any of her colleagues, so had to pretend to a kind of normality that she was far from feeling. However, the strain started to take its toll, and Anna became ill.

At first she experienced severe headaches, then her limbs started to ache and she ran a temperature. She imagined that she had flu or something similar, and thought that if she had a couple of days off work she would be alright. But she did not improve; on the contrary, she got worse. She started sweating at night, waking up in a panic, having experienced truly terrifying nightmares, in which all her children were in danger, or were taken away from her, and she was stuck, unable to move, her feet heavy, inexorably sucked down into a muddy swamp.

When her fever refused to respond to paracetemol, or any other over the counter remedies, and each day she felt weaker rather than stronger, she started to wonder whether she might possibly have malaria. She knew that once you have had malaria, the malaria parasite never leaves your system entirely, and that malaria can recur at any time when you become physically run down.

Unfortunately neither she nor Shola had any anti-malarial drugs. These had long since been used or thrown out. Anna was becoming weaker by the day, so reluctantly she decided to consult her GP, as she seemed to have no other choice. Her doctor examined her, and unfamiliar with her symptoms, and in view of Anna's insistence that she might have malaria, referred her to the local hospital for blood tests.

By the time she got to the hospital, Anna could barely stand. Her head throbbed and she was seeing everything through a mist. White uniforms came and went; no one seemed to have time to talk to her in the busy hospital, full of needy people and overstretched staff. Despite struggling unsuccessfully to remain on her feet, she collapsed in an undignified heap on the floor.

She was helped to a seat by a concerned fellow patient, and waited her turn outside the laboratory. At last she was called in, and barely able to proffer a burning arm to the waiting needle, she had samples of blood taken, by a harried looking laboratory assistant.

When the results eventually came through, Anna was told that they apparently did not show evidence of the malaria parasite. But she was convinced that she did indeed have malaria, whatever the results of the test, and was well aware that there were many different forms of the disease. She also knew, to her despair, that the medical profession in the UK was largely ignorant about malaria, something that the humblest nurse in Nigeria knew all about. When Anna persisted in asserting that she did indeed have malaria, she was told that she could not receive any treatment, until she had been over to Liverpool to see specialists in tropical medicine at the University.

By now Anna was desperate, and she feared that she might actually die before she was given the appropriate treatment. She had neither the strength nor the faith to take herself over to Liverpool, and she reflected bitterly, how ironic it would be for her to have survived hepatitis and malaria in Nigeria, to die here in the U.K. because the doctors and other medical professionals refused to listen to her. She asked the receptionist at the hospital to call a taxi to take her home, as she was totally incapable of returning by bus.

When Shola got home that evening, he could see that Anna was seriously ill, and he also recognised the symptoms of malaria. He was now convinced that this was indeed what was wrong with her. Anna was weeping hysterically and she was burning up. 'You must do something. I'm dying,' she sobbed.

Realising that the situation was desperate, he went straight back to Liverpool, without any further delay, and literally begged a pharmacist for nivaquine, the most reliable treatment for the disease. Fortunately, the man was sympathetic, and Shola returned with a precious bottle of the tablets.

Anna took the prescribed dose, rinsing down the bitter tablets with a glass of water. Like a miracle, when she woke up the next morning, her body had stopped aching, and her fever had subsided, even though she felt very nauseous because of the nivaquine. By the time she had completed the course of treatment, she was well again, even if still very weak.

※

Perhaps it was this scare that nudged Anna into action to improve her working conditions. She started to apply for jobs, spending her evenings scouring the newspapers and filling in application forms, despite her exhaustion after a hard day at work. Soon her effort was rewarded, and she was thrilled to be called for interview at the local further education college.

Anna prepared carefully for the interview. She studied the college prospectus thoroughly, as well as ensuring that she knew all about GCSE and Advanced level English syllabuses. The college campus was out in the Wirral countryside, a twenty minute trip by bus from Birkenhead. On the day of the interview, she dressed in her most respectable outfit, a grey suit she had managed to find on one of her trips to a charity shop, and a pair of new black high heeled shoes. When she got out of the bus at the end of the college drive, and looked around her, Anna felt weak with an intense longing to work in such a pleasant environment. As she walked up the long leafy drive, surrounded by trees and green open spaces, the college campus seemed almost idyllic, and so peaceful, compared to the madness of her present comprehensive in Liverpool, as well as all her previous placements.

The buildings of the college were scattered over the attractive campus, separated by grassy lawns, flower beds and shrubs, with paved paths providing access between them. Her heart sank, however, when she learned that two of the candidates for the post were internal applicants. In her heart she could not help telling herself, 'I don't know why I am putting myself through this. I've got no chance.' However, she was there now, and she might as well go through the process.

When she went in for her interview she felt that she had nothing to lose, and this feeling gave her confidence, and helped her to relax. She found herself facing three middle aged women, one being the principal of the college, a glamorous and dynamic blonde. Undeterred, she gave the interview of her life, answering every question in a positive and enthusiastic way, and emphasising her varied teaching experience and qualifications. The faces of the interviewers, though pleasant, were inscrutable, as she left the room at the end of the interview, feeling dazed and drained.

She was asked to sit and wait until the interviews were concluded, when a decision would be made and given to the candidates. As she sat there, in the waiting room, along with other hopefuls for the job, she felt empty, and was pessimistic about the outcome, because she wanted this job too much to have any chance of getting it. However she had no choice but to wait, and with a tiny part of her mind, hope too.

Eventually, one of the three interviewers returned to the waiting room, and cleared her throat importantly. The eyes of all the applicants turned to gaze at her with expectation and hope. And then Anna heard the magical words, 'Would Mrs Banjo please come back to the interview room.' She could not believe her ears: she was the one being asked back in, praised for her performance at the interview, and offered the job of lecturer.

Full of euphoria following the interview and its happy outcome, she floated down the drive to catch her bus. She could not believe that she had been so lucky. All the way home, she kept revisiting the interview in her mind, and marvelling at her good fortune. That evening Shola, Anna and Femi went out for a celebration meal. Perhaps their luck was turning at last. Anna felt as if she was in a dream, and was terrified that she would wake up to find that it was just that. However, next morning she remembered: it was really true, and she was going to work in the college.

When she told her fellow teachers at her current school that she had got a job as lecturer in a further education college, they could not believe it either. They congratulated her grudgingly, and she could tell that some of them were very envious. Why should such a nonentity get the kind of job that they would kill for?

Anna's head teacher said that she could be released from the school at half term. Anna was ecstatic with excitement and relief about her new job, and could not wait to start. Not only was it in a college, but it was also on the Wirral. She would have half her present journey time, and could get to work easily by bus. No more of the bus, train, bus that she had endured for years.

※

Teaching at the college was bliss compared to working in comprehensive schools, so much so that Anna felt that she had died and gone to heaven. The students were all sixteen plus, and even the most difficult of them were easy compared to the pupils in Knowsley. They all came from the Wirral, some from quite privileged backgrounds, and there was strong parental support; also attendance at college was an option, not a legal requirement, and so any students who were not showing sufficient commitment could be asked to leave.

Anna also now had status in the college, and was accorded respect as a lecturer, an established permanent member of staff. She had her own desk in a shared office, several free periods in each day and no yard duty! At least here her working life was bearable, and she could actually contemplate being a human being again rather than a zombie.

Even though Shola was still unhappy with his work, he managed to get by with his garden, his ironing, his records and his cannabis. The next three years were comparatively peaceful.

Taking Chances

Shade came home for the holidays; Femi continued to progress and thrive at school and Anna actually enjoyed going to college every day. She made some friends on the staff and could have a laugh with them in the staffroom at break.

Shola and Anna's relationship was not close, but they managed to get along mostly without rows. Anna learned not to question Shola when he returned late from Liverpool. She did not remonstrate with him about his cannabis or drinking. She only wanted a quiet life and it was best not to open up difficult issues. She occupied herself with putting pictures she had acquired in attic sales or second hand shops, on the walls of the house; acquiring house plants, and rummaging through charity shops, for clothes, and various odds and ends, which she arranged around the four floors of the house. Never mind that deep down she was desperately lonely. At least she was going through the motions of a happily married woman, sleepwalking through her life. As long as nothing came along to upset this equilibrium, they would be alright, or so she thought.

CHAPTER EIGHTEEN

Three years later

They had managed to get through the preceding three years without any major upsets, principally because, for most of the time, there were only three of them in the large house, and both Anna and Femi were very careful not to upset Shola if they could help it. Furthermore, Anna, Shola and Femi were all fully occupied with work and school respectively, and because they saw each other for only a limited time, mainly at the weekends, there was less chance for conflict to arise.

Femi studied hard, and Shola even allowed him to attend parties, and occasionally to entertain his friends at their own house. Perhaps this was because he subconsciously regretted his past draconian regime that had resulted in the loss of Lola, but possibly also because Femi was a boy, and he was less worried about him being exposed to other young people, and their potentially dangerous influence. Whatever the reason, discipline had been relaxed, and there was less tension and resentment in the atmosphere. However, Anna was only too well aware that Shola was still like a sleeping volcano, and equally unpredictable. It would take very little to trigger an explosion, so both she and Femi were very careful to tread carefully, to avoid any chance of trouble.

※

The postman always arrived well after Anna, Shola and Femi had left for the day. One evening when Anna got home from work, Femi handed her a letter, addressed to her in what looked like familiar handwriting, and with a local postmark. Fortunately, Shola had not yet returned from Liverpool. The letter was from Lola. Anna could feel her stomach turning over, as she wondered why her daughter had decided to make contact at this time, and hoping that nothing was wrong. None of them had heard from her directly for over two years, though they did get periodic reports of her from the Social Services. They had been informed that Lola was no longer living with the Martins but now had a flat of her own in Wallasey. She had passed two of her Advanced levels, and had been working in Liverpool in a theatre, doing some kind of administrative work, though Anna was unclear about the precise details.

She started to scan the lines of writing, hoping that perhaps Lola had finally decided to return home. It soon became clear that this was far from the case: Lola had written to tell Anna that she was pregnant, very much looking forward to having her baby, and wanting to reconcile with her mother, though not with her father, at this crucial time in her life. Anna did not know how to feel, whether happy that she would at last be able to see her daughter, or fearful for Lola's future and that of the coming baby.

'Mummy, is that letter from Lola?' Femi anxiously inquired.

'Yes. But don't say a word to your father. Lola is expecting a baby.'

'Will you go and see her?'

'Of course, but we must keep this our secret. Otherwise, you know what your father is like - he will forbid me to go.'

'You don't need to tell me that!' Femi laughed bitterly. He was well aware that they both knew better than to raise any contentious issues in front of Shola.

'She's got a flat in Wallasey. I'll write back and make an arrangement to visit her one day after college. I could go on Wednesday afternoon as I finish teaching early that day. You'll have to cover for me if I'm a bit late getting back.'

'Don't worry. Just remind me on the day, and please give Lola my love.'

Anna managed to make the necessary arrangements with Lola, and on the following Wednesday, when she had finished her teaching for the day, she travelled by bus to Wallasey. She got off the bus on the main road closest to Lola's address, which she had looked up in the A-Z. She found the house quite easily; it was one of a terrace with a small garden in front, and looked reasonably well looked after. Anna rang the bell and the door was opened by a plump elderly woman, wearing a pinafore apron over her skirt and jumper, and with her grey hair in rollers. Anna explained that she was Lola's mother. The woman regarded her with some surprise – could this middleclass white woman possibly be her tenant's mother? When she had fully registered her visitor's identity, she smiled in a friendly way.

'Lola, your mother's here,' she called up the stairs.

Anna's face was suffused with sorrow, guilt and pity, but also joy, as she hugged her daughter; Lola, for her part, was beaming. She was about seven months pregnant and looked radiant. Pregnancy suited her. She was much calmer than Anna had ever seen her, and she kept stroking her large belly with loving and proprietary caresses. She assured Anna that she had everything under control regarding the birth, as she had friends who would help her get to the hospital when she went into labour, and she was collecting clothes and other necessities for the baby.

Taking Chances

The flat was really a large bedsitting room, with cooking facilities. It was poorly furnished and in need of redecoration. Dark curtains, with a drab design, hung limply at the windows, the room was cluttered with items of clothing, books and other oddments, and the whole place appeared to Anna as dingy and depressing, like the sort of temporary accommodation allocated to refugees, on their first arrival into the country. How on earth could Lola look after a baby in these sorts of conditions?

Anna sat in the only armchair, while Lola perched on the side of the bed. She offered her mother a cup of tea, and they sat together, strange and awkward after such a long period of alienation, trying to think what to say. Anna knew that Lola was putting up a very brave front and her heart ached for her. But she dared not confide in Shola, or ask him for any help; he was just too unpredictable. All she could do at this moment was to give Lola the little money she had in her purse, and promise that she would help as much as she could.

Inevitably the subject of the father of the baby came up. Lola told her mother that he was unaware of the pregnancy, as the relationship has broken up some months previously. She was adamant that he was not to be informed. Anna discovered much later that he had forced Lola to have an abortion against her will a year earlier, so Lola's decision to go it alone became clear. At the time she was very puzzled.

'But surely he should be told. After all, it's his responsibility too.'

'No. I don't want him to know.'

'I respect your decision. But who is he? I promise I have no intention of contacting him.'

'All I can tell you is that his family is of Spanish origin, though his parents were born here.'

Anna had to leave it at that. She kissed Lola and promised to keep in touch.

'Please ask your friends to contact me if you go into labour early. I'll come and see you again the same time next week.'

All the way home on the bus Anna agonised about what she should do. She decided that she would tell Shola about Lola's pregnancy, but not about the fact that she had visited her. This proved to be the right decision as Shola, not particularly concerned at the news – he maintained that he had predicted this outcome, – categorically forbade any contact unless Lola returned to the family home.

'She will come back if you do nothing,' was all he would say.

Anna was afraid to remind him that he had said the very same thing when Lola had first left home, but their daughter had never changed her mind. Anna felt like screaming, 'It's *you* she doesn't want to see. Don't you know this even now?' but she kept silent.

Anna and Femi discussed the situation and Femi supported her decision. Anna visited Lola as often as she could in the following weeks, and gave her as much financial help as she could afford, though it was pitifully little.

❦

One day in late June, Anna received a telephone call at work. It was one of Lola's friends, Jenny.

'I'm just phoning to let you know that Lola's had a baby girl. She went into labour last night and the baby was born this morning.'

Anna felt dizzy. She thanked Jenny, found out the name of the hospital, and the ward where Lola was, and said that she would come straight away.

Anna hardly registered the hospital buildings, or how she found the maternity wing. Her heart pounded, and she felt breathless, as she climbed the stairs to the ward to which she had been directed. When she entered the maternity ward she saw Lola immediately. In Anna's eyes she was the most beautiful mother in the room. She was sitting on the side of her bed cradling a little bundle in her arms, murmuring to the newborn baby, her deep brown eyes shining with joy and relief. Her

Taking Chances

lovely coffee skin seemed to radiate warmth; her mouth beamed a loving smile, and she appeared to her mother like a modern Madonna, with her almost beatific expression.

Anna felt truly awed by the sight of her own daughter, in her newly acquired maternal role. She'll be a much better mother than I have ever been, she thought. At the same time, she feared for the vulnerability of mother and child, and wished she could help them in some meaningful way.

Lola told her that her friend, Jenny, had been with her at the birth. Again, Anna experienced a terrible sense of guilt and regret that she had not been there herself. What kind of mother was she?

When Anna had spent about an hour with her, Lola placed her little baby girl in her crib, and walked with Anna to the stairs. She looked so young, a mere child herself despite her twenty years, that Anna felt herself on the brink of tears. She held these back while she embraced her daughter and gave her a few pounds, for some necessities for herself and the baby, who was to be named Maria.

As she descended the stairs, a crushing dark cloud seemed to settle on Anna, smothering and blinding her. She felt totally lost and alone, with no one to turn to for help or even comfort. She could no longer restrain her tears, and they rolled down her face uncontrollably. She didn't care what people thought. Her failure as a mother now stared at her from every hospital wall.

But still she was inert. As she made her way home on the bus, her mind was racing, ideas and feelings tumbling through her consciousness, with no discernible direction. She had no idea what she should do, and she sensed, to her abiding shame, deep within her heart, that she would again do nothing about her marriage. She did not know which way to turn, as every option seemed fraught with danger and difficulty. Fear and secrecy reigned supreme. She was still too weak and indecisive to take any action, and it would require a sea change for her to alter the direction of her life.

CHAPTER NINETEEN

Anna did, in fact, tell Shola about Maria's birth, but she left out the fact that she had been to the hospital, giving the impression that she had received the news from one of Lola's friends. Once again he showed no real emotion, and reiterated that Lola would definitely return home, if she was not encouraged to stay away by receiving parental visits, which, according to him, would somehow sanction her independent existence.

'What do you expect me to do?' he asked in a rhetorical tone. 'She's free to come back here any time she wants.'

Anna kept silent. She knew that Lola would never again be prepared to live under the same roof as her father. But in her usual fashion, she felt it was best to avoid an argument, and then just continue to see her daughter and her baby girl in secret.

Accordingly, at the first possible opportunity, Anna made her way to the flat in Wallasey. Lola looked exhausted and drained, with large circles under her eyes. Having to manage single-handed, up half the night with a screaming baby, was taking its toll. She was, however, determinedly cheerful and full of pride. She showed off little Maria, who did not resemble anyone Anna knew. She assumed that the baby took after her father's family in appearance. Maria looked totally European; no one would ever suspect that her maternal grandfather was African. Would this be a help or a problem in her adult life? Anna wondered about this, but was unable to reach a conclusion.

Anna gave Lola as much advice on caring for babies as she remembered. She had rather blocked out the early traumatic months of her children's lives, as she had a habit of doing for anything that was stressful or difficult in her life. This had been a survival strategy she had developed over the years in order to forget past pain, and be able to cope with the present. Now she dredged her memory for tips and received wisdom about baby rearing; most of the information she had retained came from Dr Benjamin Spock and his famous baby book.

'Remember to bring up her wind after a feed. Use gripe water if she is uncomfortable. Don't be embarrassed to give her a dummy. Make sure she is changed regularly and doesn't get nappy rash.' Anna rattled off these directions, and Lola assured her laughingly that she knew all about them, and lots more.

Anna felt hollow as she left her daughter and new granddaughter. How little she could help! A few pounds here and there, and some gratuitous advice were pathetic, but Anna could still think of nothing else to do. She must maintain a home for Femi and Shade, she told herself. The fact that her marriage to Shola was now a total sham, or even an unseemly charade, still seemed immaterial; the marriage itself was immovable as a rock in her eyes.

Anna had never seriously thought about, or even dreamed of, divorce, even though she had touched on the possibility in her conversation with Dorothy. She believed, and Shola also believed, that marriage was for life, and that it must be sustained despite everything. Each time she and Shola had come to the verge of splitting up, they had always retreated from the brink. Even by this time, the real possibility of actually breaking from her husband was just not in her world or even on her horizon; she was committed to Shola and the marriage whatever happened. They had come so far and surely things could still improve. Perhaps as Shola aged he would calm down, see things in some clearer perspective, would come to some kind of self awareness. Anna still felt responsible for bringing the family to the UK, and that she owed her loyalty to Shola no matter what.

※

Anna continued to visit Lola and Maria as often as she could. After a few months they moved to a small terrace house in Birkenhead. This house would be much more suitable for a growing baby, as it had a small backyard and a separate bedroom for mother and baby. The narrow street, with its rather shabby house fronts, was not particularly attractive, but Lola made the inside of the house their own, with Maria's toys and baby equipment occupying much of the space. It had a homely feel, and conveyed a sense of freedom from constraints which Anna actually envied. Lola was free to pursue her own life and happiness in a way that was denied to her mother, albeit through her own stupidity, but her independence did subconsciously start raising awareness in Anna, of another kind of existence. Lola's new home was also in easy walking distance of the shops and other local amenities. Lola saw her friends more often now and Anna visited as and when she could manage it.

Shade had returned from Lancaster University, having gained her degree. She was now unsure about what to do next. She applied for a few jobs unsuccessfully and without enthusiasm, but eventually decided to try to get accepted on a Masters programme. She was also keen to learn to drive. Anna and Shola had not been able to afford to get a car ever since they had left Nigeria, and Shola was not keen on driving anyway. However, Anna herself was getting increasingly tired of bus queues, ordering taxis to take her home from the supermarket, and being unable to move around freely. Now under pressure from Shade, she decided to purchase a small car on hire purchase, and learn to drive again herself, as her Nigerian licence was not valid in the UK, and anyway it was long out of date.

Once she had made up her mind, Anna soon found herself in a bright new and used car showroom, with its unique and exciting smell of brand new and refurbished cars, receiving a condescending sales pitch from the brash salesman. Even being in this car sales showroom seemed to promise freedom and a new kind of life; it was like being offered the prospect of empowerment whose possibilities Anna could only dream about. Although she knew next to nothing about cars, she managed to identify a small red Nissan Micra and, after a trial run, where the salesman demonstrated the speed and other features of the car, made the necessary arrangements for buying it and having it delivered to the house, as she was not as yet licensed to drive it.

Shola was a little impressed by the arrival of the car, but was soon full of admonitions: 'Make sure you join the AA, get a lock for the gate, don't drive at night,' and other depressing warnings. Anna hoped he would keep out of it once the novelty wore off, as he had no interest in driving lessons himself.

Anna had become friendly with the mother of one of Femi's classmates. Olga was a Russian woman, of a similar age to herself, married to an English man, who looked to Anna like an aging Teddy boy or rock star. They were a very pleasant and easy going couple, and Olga had already offered to help Anna with her driving. It seemed necessary, even crucial, that Anna get her licence as soon as possible, so that she could in turn teach Shade. Driving lessons were exorbitant in price, so they hoped that they could get by with the minimum of official lessons from professional driving instructors.

Trips out at weekends with Olga became a treat for Anna. How wonderful to get away from the strained atmosphere in the house, even for a couple of hours, and just be a normal person. Sometimes she and Olga would stop in a small cafe for a coffee and chat. Anna would forget her worries and simply enjoy a momentary sense of freedom, but a sinking feeling would descend as they approached her house, and the momentary euphoria quickly evaporated.

Living in their house was like walking on a tightrope once again. Since Shade had returned home, Shola had started getting edgy, and Anna had to strain every nerve end to ensure that no rows erupted. She reminded both Shade and Femi that they absolutely must greet their father politely every morning. In his view it was an insult not to say 'Good morning, Daddy,' as soon as they saw him, and never wait to be greeted by him. Of course, this was not a difficult or unusual thing to do, whether in African or English culture. However, both children had grown to hate their father and so the greeting came out between clenched teeth. Shola, however, fortunately seemed oblivious of his children's dislike, or he chose to ignore it. Perhaps he was subconsciously afraid of triggering any more overt revelations about the true situation in the family, or he genuinely did not notice their either blank or even hostile expressions.

Shade and Femi had always been very close. When Femi was a baby Shade had looked after him like a second mother, sometimes even his real mother, when Anna was busy, preoccupied or sick. Now they found comfort in each other's company, and had once again a sibling with whom to agonise about their unhappy childhood and inadequate parents. Femi had suffered a lonely time while Shade was away at university, but now he had an ally in the house, and someone with whom to watch videos, listen to music or have discussions late into the evening. Shade had moved her bedroom up to the top floor of the house, next door to Femi, when it became clear that Lola would not be returning. On this top floor they had their own domain, as Shola seldom, if ever, ventured there.

Shola's uncertain temper was exacerbated by problems with his job. His relationship with the headmaster, Mr Mason,

Taking Chances

was invariably strained and there were constantly issues over which they clashed. Anna tried to be supportive and typed out numerous letters on his behalf regarding these various cases, and they discussed ways of resolving the problems exhaustively. Shola seemed unable to let go or concede any point, so she had to be very diplomatic in making any suggestions of compromise.

※

Shola had consistently over the years refused to even consider taking a holiday. Anna felt increasingly that both she and the children needed a break in the summer. That year she managed to get Shola to agree that she, Shade and Femi would go to Cornwall for a week, and that he would feed and water the birds while they were away. The two young people were very excited as was Anna. She did her best to conceal her own anticipation of the trip, and endeavoured to do her packing in an unobtrusive way, in case Shola changed his mind. He hated being alone at the best of times and Anna just hoped that he would survive a week without her.

Eventually the day of departure arrived, and they made good their escape without any eventualities. Anna could not believe her luck as they sat on the train speeding southwards, eating sandwiches and speculating about the holiday flat they had booked in Falmouth. The journey took a long time, but they enjoyed every minute of it, as they watched the countryside flying by. Crossing over the Tamar River, as the train negotiated the Saltash Bridge, felt like entering another country, as they left all their troubles far behind them. Even the change from their intercity train at Truro, onto a small local train that would take them to their destination on the south coast of Cornwall, was an exciting adventure.

The holiday week seemed to pass in a flash. For once Anna was free to spend time with her children without the need to constantly pander to Shola's demands. When they were at home, he showed his resentment for any time Anna devoted to either of the children, requiring all her attention for him alone. Anna, Shade and Femi explored the town, with its quaint cobbled streets, and majestic harbour, travelled to various other local beauty spots by bus or coach, spent time on Gyllyngvase and Swanpool beaches, and generally relaxed in their own safe environment. It felt wonderful to have a whole flat to themselves, where they could come and go as they pleased, eat whatever they fancied, and watch whatever they chose on television, without being answerable to anyone else, particularly not a hectoring tyrant.

On the train back to Liverpool they all felt a gloom descending and they were very quiet, willing the train to go slowly and put off the evil moment of returning home. None of them dared voice their feelings of despair and foreboding, but a sense of oppression was growing and almost palpable by the time they opened the front door.

Anna had felt a kind of premonition that all might not be well when they got back. She had telephoned Shola a couple of times during the course of the week, and he had been quite curt and unresponsive to her enquiries about his welfare. As they walked into the front hall, they all heard a loud banging and shouting from upstairs. Anna rushed up to find their bedroom door locked from the outside. Shola had insisted on new locks being fitted before she left, typical of his increasing paranoia, and he must somehow have locked himself in.

She unlocked the door with trembling hands, eventually managing to open it, to be greeted by the stench of urine and sweat. Shola was clad only in a towel, his face unshaven, and his eyes red and staring.

'What has happened? How long have you been in here?' Anna exclaimed in horror.

'I've been here since yesterday. The door locked itself from the outside. I couldn't help it. I had to urinate in the sheets. Don't look at me like that!'

Anna felt a chill run through her body. She felt sick. How could she be tied for life to such a man! Without further words, she bundled the reeking sheets into the laundry basket and headed to the basement. After she had started the washing machine, she looked around at the disgusting mess that her kitchen had become, and with a resigned sigh, she started to sort out the dirty dishes.

There appeared to be no escape. Shola seemed incapable of coping on his own; her absence for even a brief week had totally disorientated him. Anna just prayed for the time when at least the children would be independent and could make lives of their own. She could not even contemplate her own future.

The following week Shade received the offer of a place on a Masters programme in Manchester. At least she would be able to progress with her life, away from the poisonous atmosphere of the house. Femi had only two more years at school and then he too would be on his way.

'Just hang on,' Anna thought to herself. 'Just let me remain strong enough to see the children grown up and independent.' She was coming to the painful realisation that she no longer loved Shola, was even repelled by him, but as yet she could see no further than the next two years. She must ensure that Femi was able to fulfil his academic promise and gain entrance to a good university, nothing else mattered.

CHAPTER TWENTY

Two years later

Anna was now forty-nine years old, and she was internally fighting against an acceptance of her present existence, as all her life had to offer. But she had no idea of how to turn her life around, and she was experiencing periods of deep depression. Her feelings for Shola had gradually shifted from dislike to something akin to loathing. However, she still felt a kind of loyalty to him, and also a sense of obligation, as she never forgot that it was her fault that he was in the UK, and therefore subjected to racism and isolation. She sensed his mental and psychological deterioration, but could not bring herself to see it for what it was. It was too terrifying to contemplate. Sometimes she would sit on the side of the bed almost in a trance, her mind drifting into empty space, in some way trying to disassociate herself from her situation. Occasionally Shola would become aware of her silence.

Taking Chances

'What's wrong with you?' he would ask.

'Nothing,' would be her regular response and she would try to think of something innocuous to talk about.

Shola's paranoia had increased. He had always been almost pathologically afraid of outsiders: now he had taken to hanging a towel over the bathroom window in daylight, even though it had frosted glass. One day he flew into a rage because Anna corrected his positioning of the dustbin on the pavement outside the house. He had never put out the bin before, in all the years they had lived in the house. It was one of Anna's many domestic responsibilities. On this particular day, he decided for some reason that he would do it. Anna explained to him that the bin should be placed with the handle facing the street, to make it easier for the dustmen to pick it up, not the other way round. When they got back inside, Shola turned on her.

'Don't you ever dare to correct me in public again! You hopeless woman! Do you understand me?'

'Hopeless woman,' this was now a commonly used epithet for Anna: she was always a 'hopeless woman' or a 'stupid woman.' Feeling herself just that, a woman without hope, Anna just put her head down, and bore the abuse, but she hated for the children to hear it. Shola constantly insulted Anna, and made her feel unappealing and unattractive, so that she developed an inferiority complex about her appearance, especially since she had put on weight over the years. Her charity shop clothes did nothing for her self esteem, and she looked ten years older than her actual age, with the strain of her unhappy life etched on her face.

Shola's situation at school had taken a turn for the worse. His relationship with Mr Mason had become so bad as to be virtually untenable, and the headmaster was obviously looking for a pretext on which to dismiss him. Unfortunately, Shola played right into his hands.

One evening Shola returned home in a frenzied state, slamming the front door, and throwing down his bag, his face contorted with rage and anxiety.

'That's it! I'm out of that school, but I'll make sure the union force Mason to give me a reference,' he burst out.

'What do you mean? What's happened?' Anna's heart sank as she contemplated a major crisis. She knew from bitter experience that Shola could not handle stress, and that this situation would inevitably have serious repercussions for her and Femi. Shade was also due back home any day now, after the end of her course. How was she going to cope?

'All I did was call a very troublesome pupil "big ears". I only meant it as a joke, but the stupid boy took me seriously. He reported it to his parents and they went to Mason. Now apparently I have breached some major rule, and I have been suspended from work. When I think of all the racism that goes on in that place which I have been forced to overlook, all the black children who have been abused .....' Shola was overcome.

Anna did feel sincerely sorry for Shola at that moment. But she also knew that Mr Mason would not have made such an issue about this incident, if he had not had so many clashes with Shola in the past. Now he had his enemy where he wanted him, and would not let this chance slip through his fingers to rid himself and his school of an annoying thorn in his side.

The next few weeks were filled with writing letters, making phone calls, and Shola going out to meet with his union representative. The union suggested that Shola resign rather than wait to be sacked. He did attend a disciplinary hearing before the governors, but the result of this was a forgone conclusion. Mr Mason wanted him out by any means possible; it was just a question of how he would go. In the end there was a deal. It was decided that Shola would resign and would be given a reference, so that he would be able to get another teaching job.

While all this was going on Shola hardly slept, and neither did Anna. Whereas Shola normally smoked cannabis to induce

Taking Chances

drowsiness and sleep, he now felt that he needed all his faculties in order to fight his case. So he relied on ordinary cigarettes and alcohol to dull his pain, but it was not enough. This resulted in violent outbursts. He might throw this plate of food at the wall if Anna annoyed him in any way, or he would threaten to leave the house and find another woman. Anna sincerely wished he would do just that, and leave her in peace, or that preferably he would walk under a bus.

In the midst of all this confusion, Shade returned home with her Masters degree, at the worst period that she could possibly have returned to the troubled family. Although she spent most of her time in her room applying for jobs, she inevitably came into contact with her father. For many years now, neither Femi nor Shade had actually had a conversation with their father. He talked at them, and they replied in monosyllables. Anna tried very hard to act as intermediary so as to prevent Shola noticing that the children were unwilling to communicate with him. Now it seemed that Shola was gradually becoming conscious of Shade's feelings about him; he tended to overlook Femi in all this, just as he had throughout his son's childhood. Anna was aware that it would only be a matter of time before Shola started picking on Shade again, and that this time she would have to act.

Femi had been accepted at Cambridge, where he was going to read Modern Languages. Shola had wanted him to study Law, the legal profession having high status in Nigeria, and there had been several arguments about the matter. Eventually Shola had agreed to Femi's choice of degree, on condition that he should take a Law conversion course when he graduated. Meanwhile, during the summer holidays, whilst waiting for his Advanced level exam results, Femi was to go on a trip to Greece with some of his fellow pupils and their Classics teacher.

Now the day had arrived for Femi to depart for Greece. Although Anna was glad for the boy to be able to get away from the tension in the house, she feared for herself and Shade, being left with Shola in his present state of mind. Femi had always acted as a buffer. Perhaps Shola was in some sense conscious that Femi was fast becoming a man, almost as tall as his father, who might be pushed into standing up to him, if he bullied the women too outrageously. Anna had been terrified at the idea of just such an eventuality, with her son and her husband coming to physical blows. But now she felt that they were just too vulnerable without his protection.

Anna was preparing to take Femi by car to his pick up point for the airport. They were already running late because Shola kept asking Anna to help him with this and that. As they were about to leave the house, Shola called Anna, loud urgency in his voice.

'Come and help me tie up this cucumber plant. It must be done immediately or the plant will be ruined.'

'I can't. We haven't got time. I'll help when I get back.'

'It's got to be done now.'

For one of the few times in her entire marriage, Anna ignored Shola's protests and almost ran to the car with Femi. She knew she would have to face a scene when she returned, but she had no choice. Fortunately, they made it to meet the other travellers just in time. Femi was the last to arrive at the agreed departure venue, the house of one of his friends. As they zoomed into the drive, they could see parents and boys milling around in front of the house, laden with luggage. The organiser of the trip, Femi's classics teacher was very relieved to see him, so that the party was complete and they could set off for the airport. Anna embraced her son, told him not to worry, and that she would be able to fix things with his father.

She wished she was as sure of this as she pretended, and waved goodbye to her darling boy with a smiling face. Inside she was full of dread. She felt that her marriage was sliding helter skelter towards disaster and she had no way of stopping it, and she was not sure that she really wanted to. She was just terrified about how it would end, as she would never be able to discuss their problems with Shola in a calm manner. Would someone get physically hurt? She could not imagine separating from Shola without violence, the violence he threatened verbally on an almost daily basis.

'I'll cut you into little pieces' or 'I will do like Marvin Gaye's father,' were two of his many alarming threats, which were calculated to terrify them all, and succeeded in doing so.

Shola refused to speak when she returned. He was capable of giving her the silent treatment for several days after a row. Anna crept up to Shade's room and told her what was going on, and she too became full of dread. Shola was now very volatile, and they knew that anything could happen, when he was in this kind of mood. Over recent weeks, he had become suspicious and jealous if they went out together in the car. He had imposed strict rules about when they had to be back, and on no account were they allowed to be out after dusk.

After a couple of days Shola started speaking again, but it had been better when he was silent. He constantly criticised either Anna or Shade. He flew into a rage if his food was not ready when he wanted it. He threatened to burn Anna with the iron he was using to press his clothes, when she stupidly asked him what was wrong. The volcano was about to erupt but she had no way of knowing when this would be, or whether she and Shade would escape alive.

CHAPTER TWENTY-ONE

The next night Anna tossed and turned in the large bed upstairs, fearful of all the terrifying scenarios her fevered imagination presented to her, while Shola slept on the sofa in the sitting room. This seemed to Anna ominous as he very seldom did this, and it always heralded a major outburst. Usually Shola was insistent that they slept together; in spite of Anna's growing revulsion, their weekly pattern of sexual relations continued as normal. Anna used to turn off mentally, and think about chores she had to do or errands she had to run. Shola seemed oblivious to her 'absence', and continued to use sex as way of releasing his stress, and also exerting his power in the relationship. She seldom denied him in fear of what the reprisals might be. At the least Shola would be in a foul temper, while at worst he might become violent.

When Anna woke up the next morning, and registered Shola's absence from his side of the bed, everything that had happened the previous day came back to her. She quickly slipped on some clothes, and went quietly down stairs. She looked round the sitting room door in dread, wondering what would confront her. She was prepared for anything, and somewhere in her subconscious, she felt ready to act in an independent and resolute way, which would have been unthinkable even a few months previously.

To her surprise, Shola greeted her normally, but then proceeded to list a series of complaints about Shade. Anna was filled with foreboding, and knew as he spoke, vehemently and angrily, that she would now be forced to do something drastic. Shola was obviously going to revert to his constant picking on their daughter, now that she was living at home once again, and from her knowledge of her husband, and his modes of behaviour, she could sense that he was looking for a major confrontation with his elder daughter, probably that very day. His reference to Shade as 'That Shade' had terrifying resonances from the past.

Not again, she said to herself. I may have been too weak to do anything in the past, but I am not going to lose another daughter. She was increasingly in dread that Shola was going vent all his frustration on Shade, just as he had when she was a child, even though she was now a grown woman. He would definitely drive Shade from the house, one way or the other, whether by a violent verbal attack or, the most horrific scenario, God forbid, even physical aggression, which was something that she could not even contemplate. Shade had always been a scapegoat for the malaise of the family, and Anna could sense that Shola now more than ever needed a scapegoat.

Anna had never considered herself a devious person, but the experience of years of hiding things from her husband was now going to be of vital importance. In her mind, full of fevered fear and horrific imaginings, it might even make the difference between life and death. She must protect her daughter at all costs, and she also realised that she no longer cared about the marriage that she had struggled to maintain for twenty-six long years. She determined that she was going to take swift evasive action, while the volcano was still rumbling threateningly below the ground, sending up its occasional showers of red hot lava, but not yet bursting out violently enough to endanger the lives of the inhabitants of the surrounding towns and villages.

With all these thoughts rushing through her head, Anna's first thought was that she must try to pacify her husband, and lull him into a belief of her solidarity with him. Accordingly, she nodded at Shola's complaints, 'Yes, I can see what you mean,' and she smiled, pretending to agree with him, and then said that she would go and make some breakfast. Before she went down to the kitchen, however, she slipped upstairs and woke Shade.

She had no time to explain what was going on.

'Shade, wake up. Get dressed, but don't come down until I tell you.'

Shade realised that something serious was about to happen. She needed no second warning, but immediately started to pull on her clothes.

Anna sped down to the kitchen and, with trembling hands, cooked some eggs for Shola, made him a cup of coffee and some toast, and then put all the breakfast things on a tray. Trying her best to look normal, she took them up to the sitting room. Shola had started on his interminable ironing, and playing his records at full blast. For once Anna was glad to hear the din, as it would drown out any other sounds, such as Shade coming downstairs.

There was no time to lose in giving Shade any further details. She crept up to her daughter's room and told her to come down straight away, and that they were going shopping. Shade tiptoed down silently, carrying only a small handbag.

Anna put her head round the sitting room door.

'I'm going to the supermarket with Shade. We'll be back in a couple of hours.'

Shola seemed to be preoccupied with his own thoughts. He nodded absently.

Taking Chances

Anna almost bundled Shade out of the house, terrified that Shola would somehow come out and challenge them, like the mythical giant Cyclops, threatening Odysseus and his men. He did not appear; Anna and Shade got into the car calmly as if nothing was wrong. In fact, Shade was still oblivious to the real state of affairs, and she had no way of knowing that her mother's state of mind and resolve had changed radically overnight, and that change had been confirmed by her conversation with Shola that morning.

Once she had backed the car out of the drive, Anna drove to the supermarket as if all the demons of hell were at her back. She parked in the Tesco car park and started trembling violently. She had no plan apart from the determination that she was not going back to the house. Although no scheme had been conceived or verbalised, yet she was sure of that much.

'Mummy, are you ok? What's going on?' asked Shade anxiously.

Anna did not reply directly. Instead she looked steadily at her daughter, and quietly asked her, 'Do you want to go back?'

Shade did not hesitate for a second. 'No. Do you want to?'

Anna burst into tears. Great wracking sobs forced their way through her whole body, and she leaned on the steering wheel, oblivious to the stares of any passersby. After a few minutes, when the spasm of weeping had subsided, she spoke tonelessly but firmly:

'No. We're not going back. I need to think about what we will do, but nothing will make me set foot in the house again while your father is there.'

Anna did not tell Shade about her father's threats against her. She did not want to scare her unnecessarily now that they had escaped.

Instead she dried her eyes and said, 'Let's go and have some breakfast in the cafeteria. We'll try to think of something.'

Over coffee and croissants, Anna and Shade tried to think of where they could find refuge for a few days, while they decided what to do in the longer term. They only had the clothes they stood up in, and the car. Anna suddenly remembered that they had booked a holiday flat in South Wales for the week after Femi got back from Greece. This meant that they had a week's accommodation already paid for, and they would still have time before they went on holiday to arrange longer term accommodation for their return.

'If we can just find somewhere for about ten days before we go to Wales we will be ok. I don't want to descend on Lola and the baby. She has very little space and enough problems of her own. I'll get in touch in a day or two and see if she knows of anywhere we could stay for a week. In the meantime, let's go and see my friend, Dorothy, in Liverpool. Perhaps she can put us up for a couple of days.'

Shade had not seen Dorothy for a number of years, indeed, she hardly remembered her, but she agreed with Anna that it was probably the best option in this emergency situation. Femi was due back in about three days, and they would have to find another solution by that time.

They got back in the car and Anna drove them, almost by instinct, because she could not clearly remember the route, to the small house in Liverpool where Dorothy lived. They had kept in touch over the years but she had not seen her friend recently.

Anna parked her car opposite the house, and she and Shade walked up to the front door and knocked. Dorothy opened the door. She had only to look at Anna's tearstained face to realise that something was very wrong. She smiled at Shade and put her arms round Anna, drawing her into the living room. Ray and the children were out so there was no need for any pretence or shyness. The warmth of Dorothy's welcome, and her kindness started Anna's tears again. Sitting on the sofa next to Shade, in between sobs, she tried to tell Dorothy about the situation and Shade added details when her mother became totally incoherent.

'Of course you can stay here for a few days. We haven't got much room but you are very welcome. I have never forgotten how you helped me in Jos, and this is my chance to try to pay back something of the debt I owe you. But what are you going to do about your clothes?'

'I don't know. I can't go back there.'

'You'll have to get the police to escort you. They will if you are afraid of violence.'

'I can't use the police against Shola. I know how racist they are. How can I do that to him?'

'What about what he is doing to you and the children? Anyway, we'll ask Ray's advice when he gets back.'

Anna collapsed on the sofa, overcome with the events of the day. Dorothy drew Shade into the kitchen with her, and Anna was vaguely aware of them talking quietly in the next room. She had no idea what she was going to do, but she did know that she had come to a turning point in her life. She had tried to leave Shola several times before, only to end up going back to him. She felt certain that this time it had to be different. She was now nearly fifty years old, almost half a century. Could she spend the rest of her life in such a destructive relationship? Would it even be fair to Shola to continue living with a woman who had come to hate and despise him? She also knew, beyond all doubt, that this time she would have to choose between Shola and the children. She had already lost Lola, and definitely she would lose Shade and Femi also, if she remained with Shola, even if they all survived physically.

When Dorothy came back into the sitting room, as if reading her mind, she sat down beside Anna and took her hands in hers. She looked directly into Anna's tearstained eyes, and said, quietly and firmly, 'You have your chance. Now take it!' Anna would remember these words in the days and weeks ahead, and whenever she weakened or felt bitterly sorry for Shola, they would re-echo in her mind and fortify her will to end her marriage.

Later in the afternoon, Anna telephoned Lola and explained what had happened. Lola was incredulous, but agreed to ask her friends if they knew of a flat Anna could rent for when Femi returned from Greece. She naturally felt rather bitter that Anna had made this decision so long after her own departure from the family. What could Anna say? She just knew that she was now strong enough, or desperate enough, to make a decision which should have been made years earlier.

Once away from his threatening presence, Anna could feel sorrow for what Shola had become. A very volatile and paranoid temperament, combined with the effects of racism and years of disappointment, had made Shola what he was today. How different from the handsome and charismatic young man she had married! How full of hope they had been in the early months of their marriage; they had been prepared to take on the world. But gradually their love and optimism had been eroded. Coming to the UK had probably exacerbated the process, but it might have come to the same ending even if they had remained in Nigeria. Anna could not help wondering how Shola would cope without her. She had, in a sense, shielded him from the day to day demands of survival, though she had not been able to prevent him from losing his job. But she had to focus on the present crisis. She had Shade and Femi to think of; they would need somewhere to live. Most urgently, she and Shade needed their possessions, particularly now a change of clothes. How was she going to be able to retrieve these?

When Ray arrived home, Dorothy quickly outlined what was happening.

Ray was completely on Anna's side. He was outraged when he heard about the violence, and threats of violence to which she and Shade had been subjected.

'You will have to contact the police and ask them to go with you to the house. It's their job to help in cases like this.'

'But how can I use the police against him? It's his worst fear, and I have always agreed with him that the police are racist.

Now I will be using my white skin to get the police on my side while, they label him a savage black brute.'

'He's actually behaving like one,' replied Ray. 'I'm a black man myself, but I would be ashamed to victimise a helpless woman and children, regardless of colour. You've really got no choice. Anyway, the police won't do anything to him unless he gets violent, and I don't think he will be stupid enough to attack anyone if they are there.'

Anna thought about what Ray had said, and eventually agreed that he was probably right. With shaking hands she picked up the telephone and called the Merseyside police. She felt ashamed to be in such a situation, and a traitor to Shola, but it seemed the only thing she could do. She certainly could not risk going to the house on her own, or even with friends. Anything might happen with Shola in his present state, and it was not worth the risk. By now he would have realised that she and Shade were not coming back, and she dreaded to think what was going through his mind.

Despite her protests, Shade had insisted on accompanying her to the house, and now the two of them sat with Dorothy and Ray, waiting for the arrival of the police in a state of fear and apprehension.

CHAPTER TWENTY-TWO

Within twenty minutes, a police car had pulled up at Dorothy and Ray's house, its lights flashing. A policeman and a policewoman came up the path and knocked at the door. Anna could hardly focus on their faces, and all she noticed was that the policewoman was blonde and sturdy, with her police cap perched on her hair, which was caught up in a neat bun. The man did not register at all – he was just a policeman. Both the officers had busy walkie-talkies, which buzzed and whined alarmingly, with the distant crackling of disembodied voices. There was a brief discussion about the situation, involving Dorothy and Ray as well as Anna and Shade. In fact, by this time anxiety and fear had rendered Anna almost speechless, so it was left to the others to outline events to the two police officers.

Soon Anna and Shade were speeding towards Birkenhead, in the back of the police car. As they approached their road, Anna felt as if she was going to vomit. She had no idea what to expect; she hoped and prayed that Shola would let them into the house without putting up any kind of resistance. The house itself loomed large and dark, with a light on only in the front sitting room.

The police officers told Anna and Shade to wait in the car while they spoke to Shola. Anna could hear them first knocking at the door, and then having a brief conversation with Shola. He seemed at first unwilling to let them in, but the police must have used some persuasive tactics, for soon they were signalling for Anna and Shade to come into the house.

Shola was standing in the hall looking defensive and also alarmed. Anna told Shade to go up to her room, and bring down some changes of clothing and underwear, and any other necessities she felt she would need in the next few days. She herself went up to the bedroom and grabbed a few pieces of clothing. She did not really know what to take, as she was not actually thinking at all. Her mind was consumed by images of Shola beleaguered and impotent, downstairs with the vigilant police officers.

Suddenly Shola was behind her, and she was aware that the policeman was also in the room. She turned and looked at the distorted, yet all too familiar, face of her husband. He looked as if he was about to collapse. She had never seen him this vulnerable before, except perhaps after the death of this father. Before she could say anything, he was on his knees, clutching at her skirt, flecks of spittle dribbling from the corners of his mouth.

'Anna, I beg you. Don't leave me. I promise I won't harm you or Shade.'

Anna experienced intense pity for this broken man, her husband. Her resolve almost weakened but she remembered Dorothy's words: 'You have your chance. Now take it!' She also recalled Shola's brutality, especially to the children.

'I'm sorry. I have to go,' she whispered, shaking her skirt free from his clinging hand.

She felt like Judas, but she had no choice.

She descended the stairs, a travel bag of clothing and toiletries in her hand, followed by Shola and the police officer. The other officer was in the hallway, speaking into her walkie-talkie. Shade also arrived in the hall at that moment, carrying a small bag of her possessions. Despite her fear, she looked cool and determined. Shola hissed at her, 'You are a wicked girl. It's your fault. You are breaking up a marriage of twenty-six years.'

Anna took Shade's hand, and pulled her away to the safety of the waiting police car. They had just a few clothes, and Anna knew that it would be some time before they would be able to return for the rest of their possessions. They were leaving their home, and facing the unknown outside world, an uncaring world, with all its dangers and cruelty; yet their home was an even more dangerous place for them now, and they had to take their chances outside.

It was late by this time. The night was dark though mild. They left Shola in his now deserted and empty house, a lonely and embittered man, with no company apart from the birds in their cages in Femi's room, and sped through the Mersey tunnel back to Liverpool and the warmth and domestic peace of Dorothy and Ray's happy home.

That night Anna wept until she had no tears left. She wept for herself, for Shola and for the children. She wept for what she felt was a wasted life, a spoilt life. What was left of the dreams with which they had started out? Her face was hot. Scalding tears drenched the pillow which rested her weary head, in the little bedroom that Dorothy had cleared for Anna and her daughter. Shade and Dorothy murmured near her, but Anna felt that she was floating away from everything that was familiar into an unknown land. She felt as if she was mourning a death, the death of her marriage and everything that she had tried to achieve for the past twenty-six years. Later she would be able to reassess her life, to feel some relief at her newly acquired freedom, but now she must mourn, she must release in tears the accumulated grief of her failures and disappointments. Nothing and no-one could comfort her that night.

※

When Anna awoke from a troubled and fitful sleep, she was bewildered. Where was she? She felt as if a heavy weight was pressing down on her chest, and she found it difficult to breathe. Gradually, the events of the previous day came back to her with sickening clarity, and she looked round for Shade and then at her watch. It was almost ten o'clock. Shade must have crept silently out of the bedroom without waking her.

As Anna tried to get up, she was aware of a throbbing in her head, and her eyes felt sore and swollen. She had fallen asleep in her clothes, and now she felt dirty and uncomfortable. She crept over to the dressing table and looked at herself in the mirror. An unknown creature looked vacantly back at her. Its eyes were red and puffy, its face blotchy and its expression blank.

I must pull myself together, she admonished herself. There's so much to be done. Femi will be back in a couple of days and I've got to find a place to stay by that time.

After she had found the bathroom and splashed water on her face, Anna started to feel a bit more human, but still totally disorientated. She made her way downstairs, to find Dorothy and Shade sitting at the kitchen table finishing their breakfast.

Both of them jumped up when they saw Anna. They hugged her, and sat her down at the table. Dorothy put on the kettle for some coffee, and asked Anna what she would like to eat.

'Thanks, but I don't feel like eating anything. I feel really sick,' she replied.

'You must keep your strength up,' insisted Dorothy and proceeded to make Anna a piece of toast to eat with her coffee.

Anna did feel slightly better after her breakfast, but she was constantly aware of a hollow place inside. What was she doing here? How was she going to cope with the situation? She had

Shade, and soon Femi too, relying on her. She must be sensible and make the right decisions for their future.

She decided to telephone Lola. Lola had some good news.

'I've spoken to some friends of mine. They just happen to have an empty flat which you can rent for a week.'

She then proceeded to give Anna the details about the rent, and how she could get hold of the key.

'We're so grateful for your help, Lola.'

'It's ok,' replied Lola. 'I couldn't very well let my mother and siblings sleep on the street. But I hope that you remember how I have been treated by this family, and see that I am being kinder to you than you ever were to me.'

'I know,' said Anna humbly. 'I won't ever forget it.'

Anna and Shade were pressed by Dorothy to stay with her family another night, and then it was agreed that they would go back to Birkenhead and move into the flat which Lola had found for them. It was also necessary that they inform Mrs Mortimer, the mother who was going to pick up Femi from the airport, along with her own son, to take him directly to her house, and under no circumstances drop him at their old home. Anna would then pick him up from there.

The following day, after thanking Dorothy and Ray profusely for their kindness and hospitality, and receiving hugs and assurances of their continuing support, Anna and Shade climbed into the red Micra with their pitifully few belongings, and headed back through the Mersey tunnel to the Wirral.

They soon located the promised flat and picked up the keys from Lola's friend. The flat was only a few streets away from their old house, and they were very anxious to avoid Shola. They felt like fugitives, which in fact they were, as they parked far away from the flat, and looked over their shoulders constantly whenever they went out. The flat itself was in a good respectable, tree lined street. It was on the ground floor, and spacious, with two bedrooms, and a well furnished attractive lounge, and modern kitchen and bathroom. It was fairly clean generally, but

Taking Chances

the bedding was disgusting, and the sink was full of dirty dishes. Anna washed the dishes, and then stripped the beds completely. She would have to purchase some minimal bed covers, as there was no way they could even attempt to wash and re-use the linen they had found there. It was lucky that it was summer and still quite warm at night.

Anna and Shade slept alone in the flat the first night, each trying to cheer and reassure the other, but both were desperately looking forward to Femi arriving back the next day.

'What do you think Femi will think about all this?' Anna asked Shade as they ate their breakfast.

'He'll be very pleased that you finally made the decision to leave. He and I have often talked about the idea, but we had given up hope that you would ever have the courage to make a move. But Mummy, we can't leave Femi's birds in that house! They might die, if they don't get their seed and water. We'll have to get them before Femi gets back.'

Anna had been quietly thinking the same thing. But how were they going to get into the house without Shola being around, and actually go up to Femi's room and retrieve the birds in their cages? It looked impossible. However Anna remembered the saying that 'desperate diseases require desperate remedies,' and made up her mind that they must at least attempt to rescue the birds. So she and Shade hatched a plan.

They parked their car in an inconspicuous place, about two hundred yards from their old home, so that they could keep watch, without being seen. Luck was on their side, and after about half an hour, they saw Shola leaving the house, dressed smartly in a suit and marching up the road, in the opposite direction to where they were parked, in a purposeful way.

They allowed about ten minutes to make sure he did not return for anything he might have forgotten, and then, like characters in a crime movie, moved the car to the front of the house. Shade was left in the car to keep watch, with instructions to press loudly on the horn if there was any sign of Shola returning. Anna sped up the steps to the front door, inserted her key, and flew up the stairs to Femi's room. The birds were there, happily singing away; obviously Shola had been looking after them, keeping them supplied with seed and fresh water. Anna seized the two cages, and half ran from the room and down the stairs, trying not to spill the water containers and seed trays over the floor as she went. All the time she was doing this, she felt herself trembling and her hands shook. What would happen if Shola came back unexpectedly and found her there in the house? The prospect was too awful to contemplate.

Anna shot out of the house, a birdcage in each hand, thrust the cages onto the back seat of car, jumped into the driver's seat and they sped off. Their mission had been accomplished. After they got back to their flat and they had stopped shaking, Anna and Shade congratulated each other on their foolhardy, but ultimately successful enterprise. There was an amusing aftermath, which Anna did not find out until she returned to work in September. A laughing administrator informed her that Shola had telephoned the college to complain that Anna had broken in and stolen the birds from his house.

'What did he expect us to do about it?' she chuckled. By that time, even Anna could see the funny side of the incident.

※

Anna could not wait for her son to return, as they really needed his support now. Even though he was only seventeen, Femi was mature beyond his years, possibly in part because of all those years as a 'latch key kid', and also from learning to survive and succeed, despite his dysfunctional family, and she knew that she and Shade would feel much more secure to have him around.

She also realised that she would have to allay his fears about his university fees and maintenance, and resolved to contact the Local Education Authority without delay to explain their change of circumstances, and apply for a grant. Dorothy and

Taking Chances

Ray had also advised Anna to contact a lawyer, and she resolved that she would do both these things as soon as Femi returned.

Now they just had to wait until the afternoon when they would be reunited, and the three of them could make plans for the future together. Anna had telephoned Mrs Mortimer, the previous day, and asked her to take Femi directly to her house from the airport, where she would be meeting both boys. She was obviously curious about the change of arrangement, but Anna promised to explain when they picked up Femi. She also wanted to be the one to tell him about what had happened.

It's only a few more hours and we will have Femi with us, Anna said to herself, her heart lightening at the thought. She would not rest now until her beloved son was back safely with them, and they would be able to feel like a family again.

CHAPTER TWENTY-THREE

Femi was looking out for them when they arrived at the Mortimers' bungalow, which was situated in an affluent area of Heswall, one of the better off small towns on the Wirral. The bungalow was large, set in attractively laid out gardens, and was accessed by a sweeping gravel drive. All the houses on the exclusive estate were immaculate in appearance, and the whole neighbourhood looked like a spread in 'Homes and Gardens', or alternatively, a life like set for a glossy American soap. How could people, who dwelt in houses such as these, have any idea about what it was like to live in the real world? Anna wondered.

She was overwhelmingly relieved to see Femi's familiar, handsome and much loved face, tanned after his holiday in Greece, wearing shorts and a white tee-shirt, covered in Greek characters. These proved to be a quotation from the famous Cretan writer, Nikos Kazantzakis, which Anna later found translated as: 'I do not hope for anything; I am not afraid of anything. I am free.' When she thought about these words, she felt that if she could live by them, she might indeed find salvation.

Now Femi rushed out to meet Anna and Shade as they got out of the car.

'What's happening, Mummy?' he asked as he hugged them.

'We'll explain everything later,' replied Anna, as she embraced her son.

'We've left home,' added Shade, before Anna could say any more.

'Don't worry about anything. We've got somewhere to stay for now, but we couldn't risk you going to the house. There has been a huge row and your father is on his own there now,' Anna whispered, unwilling for the whole extent of their dire situation to be known by the Mortimers.

Mrs Mortimer, a matronly well dressed blonde woman, called to them from the doorway.

'Come in and have a cup of tea.'

They accepted politely, although this was the last thing they wanted at this point, to have to pretend normality, when the three of them knew that they were going through a momentous change in all of their lives.

Anna thanked Mrs Mortimer for looking after Femi, and explained simply that she had decided to leave her husband, and that she and the two children were staying temporarily in a flat in Birkenhead. They escaped as soon as they could, and drove back to their little haven. Anna was glad that at least they had a roof over their heads, and that she was not putting Femi through the sense of homelessness that she and Shade had experienced for the first few days of their flight.

When she got up the next morning, Anna decided that she had to tackle three major issues: she had to consult a lawyer about her marital situation; go to the Education Office about Femi's university grant; and try to find a house to rent for when they got back from Wales.

In the event, these three projects took the best part of the six days that they had left, before they were due to travel to Wales. The Education Office was quite straightforward: Anna was given some forms to fill in to register her change of status and to apply for a grant on Femi's behalf. On the other hand, the visit to the lawyer proved to be traumatic.

Anna found a solicitor quite randomly, by looking in the Yellow Pages for a legal firm on the Wirral, which dealt with family issues. The office felt rather gloomy despite its comfortable chairs and glossy brochures, which Anna registered while sitting in the waiting room. She soon found herself seated opposite a young, attractive and business like Asian woman, who did not seem much older than Shade. In the lawyer's office, her eyes scanned the heavy legal tomes and filing cabinets, and her heart sank. She felt deeply humiliated to have to detail the unpleasant and degrading aspects of her marriage in this formal situation, and to such a young woman. She was also extremely conscious of being dressed in the same inappropriate, and now grubby, clothes for the past week.

She started to catalogue some of Shola's behaviour that had forced her to leave him, but she had only mentioned about three items on her long mental list, when the lawyer stopped her.

'In my opinion, you have more than enough evidence from what you have told me already, to file for a divorce, on the grounds of unreasonable behaviour.'

Anna felt shocked: it started to dawn on her that she had been living in an unreal world, believing that her marriage, though stormy, was in some degree normal. She realised that she had been desperately hanging on, probably because Shola was African, giving him the benefit of the doubt that she would never have given a white man. Her sense of responsibility for his being in the UK at all, had blinded her to the reality of his pathological behaviour.

Still she hesitated. 'I think I would prefer to go for a legal separation.'

Taking Chances

The lawyer replied quickly. 'I really do advise you to opt for a divorce. It will save a lot of time and money, as it will probably come to that in the end anyway.'

Anna thought for a moment. She mentally replayed and reviewed the years of her marriage. However hard she tried, she could not think of a single reason to stay married to Shola. Yes, it was over.

'Alright, I will go for a divorce,' she sighed.

They discussed the house. The lawyer insisted that Anna had a right to the house as she had an under age son, but Anna was unsure. She knew that Shola would fight to keep it, and she was not sure whether she would want to live there even if he left. She felt that he would not stay away from them if he knew where they were. She left this issue in the air, and agreed that the lawyer should write to Shola, to see what he wanted to do about their home.

The next thing that had to be done urgently was to find some more permanent accommodation for them when they got back from Wales. How convenient that they had booked this holiday several months previously! It would provide them with a much needed breathing space, while the formalities for renting a house could be carried out.

Anna, Shade and Femi had been to visit Lola in her little terrace house. Lola was ambivalent about their situation. On one hand she was happy that they had finally followed her lead and left their father; on the other, she felt aggrieved that she had been left to struggle alone, when the other three had each other. She did, however, warn Anna to be careful about where she decided to live.

Lola was very much 'into' the supernatural or paranormal, and set great store by tarot cards and other fortune telling practices. Now she got out her tarot cards, gravely laid them out on the floor and gave Anna a reading, whilst the other two looked on with both scepticism and interest.

'The cards are telling you to move as far away from Birkenhead as possible,' she revealed.

Anna did not need to be convinced about this. It was in tune with her survival instincts as well. Both Shade and Femi emphatically agreed. The last thing any of them wanted was to find Shola knocking on their door.

Accordingly, she drove over to Ellesmere Port, on the other side of the Wirral, quite close to Chester. She went into an estate agent's office which had details of houses for rent in its window. She was taken to view a couple of properties: one was impossible, in terribly bad condition, with broken windows and an overgrown garden. The other was a nondescript ex-council house on a red brick estate in Ellesmere Port. It did not look highly inviting, but Anna felt that she had little choice in agreeing to rent it on a six month lease. She simply did not have time, or the energy, to search for anything more congenial. At least it was only temporary, and they could make more permanent arrangements later. Accordingly she paid a deposit, and left the agent to take up her references, and they fixed a date for them to move in, the day that they would be returning from their holiday.

Anna arranged to leave her car and the birds with a colleague from work, who happened to live near the college, and also not far from Ellesmere Port, while she went down to Wales. Soon the day arrived when they were due to leave for their fortuitous holiday. They cleared the rented flat, and made sure they left it in much better condition than they had found it. Anna loaded the car with their few possessions, and the two bird cages, and drove it to her colleague's house. Then she, Shade and Femi made their way to Liverpool and the train for Wales.

Safely aboard the train, as it pulled away from the platform at Lime Street station, Anna, Shade and Femi breathed a collective sigh of relief. For a week at least, they could get away from the pressing problems of readjusting to a new life, and relax in a holiday environment far away from the traumas of the past ten days.

The train raced and rattled its way south. Shade and Femi chatted and laughed together like school children on an outing. They thoroughly enjoyed the freedom of travel, purchasing sandwiches and soft drinks from the buffet car, looking out of the carriage windows at the fields and houses flying by.

Anna watched them absently, absorbed in her own thoughts. How happy they were away from the malignant atmosphere of their old home! She should have made a move years ago. But how strange to be going away on holiday when her marriage had broken up less than two weeks previously! It seemed almost surreal, but what an opportune break for them all.

Anna thought about her mother; she had phoned her a few days previously, to tell her about her split with Shola. She had not expected much sympathy or support, and so she was not disappointed by her mother's negative reaction to her news. Even though her mother had always disapproved of her marriage, and had never got on with Shola, on the rare occasions that she had seen him, now she made it clear that, in her opinion, she considered that Anna had been too hasty in ending their relationship. Divorce was anathema to her, almost on a par to her revulsion at her daughter's marriage to an African in the first place. She saw Anna as bringing fresh shame on her, and urged her to return to her husband before it was too late. She was not interested in hearing Anna's account of what had gone on, and held to the view that Anna had made her bed, and must therefore lie on it for the rest of her life. There was no help or even advice to be had from her, and Anna knew that she would have to deal with her problems on her own.

When they arrived in Tenby, a place totally unknown and strange to them, they got a taxi to their holiday home. The landlady was there to greet them and hand over the keys. It was a very comfortable terrace house, clean and bright, and it was all theirs. They had absolute freedom with no one to shout at them, threaten dire consequences and cast a shadow over all their hopes and dreams. The little house was well furnished, and upstairs boasted a modern shiny bathroom, and two good sized bedrooms. Anna shared the larger twin bedded room with Shade, while Femi occupied the smaller room on his own. Downstairs there was a cosy lounge with a television, as well as a comfortable sofa and armchairs, and a cheerful kitchen dining room. The house was in the centre of the town, so it was convenient for the shops, and it was also a very short walk to the beach.

Tenby was such a pretty seaside town, looking like the proverbial picture postcard resort, with its houses painted bright pastel shades, and the long sandy beach providing space for walking, paddling and picnicking. The sand was soft to their bare feet, and stretched around the coastline in a golden brown carpet as far as their eyes could see, and the blue sea broke on the shore in gentle white surf. It seemed idyllic after the disturbing and painful events they had just experienced. There was also a quaint little harbour nestled in a peaceful protected rocky basin, adjacent to the beach, but feeling like the living heart of the town, with brightly coloured boats bobbing at anchor within it, and pastel coloured tall houses looking down on it from three sides.

The three of them even took a boat trip in a small craft, skimming over the calm sea, to Caldey Island, where there was a famous male monastery forbidden to women. Femi, being male, was allowed in as a member of a guided tour, but said nonchalantly afterwards that there was nothing very special about it, apart from the monks carrying out their everyday activities. Anna and Shade were quite disappointed to hear this as they, along with a group of other excluded women, waited curiously, sitting on the grassy garden outside the monastery, to hear about the wonders to be revealed to their men folk.

Later, they all explored the beautiful island, walking along the cliffs, gazing at the view from the promontory, where a

Taking Chances

picturesque white lighthouse overlooked the blue sea. They had tea seated outside at a wooden table, in a flower filled, sweet smelling garden, bees buzzing, small birds chirping, and gulls wheeling over head. Having taken numerous photographs, and armed with souvenirs bought from the monastery shop, they returned over the rippling blue waves to Tenby.

The weather was glorious, with the sun shining every day in a cloudless blue sky. This break was such a needed bonus for them all, and provided a solace to their battered spirits.

Not everything was harmonious, however.

One evening, in an attempt to break away from the stilted and formal customs of the past, Anna suggested that perhaps now they were grown-up, the children might like to call her by her first name. She had not really thought the idea through, but she had noticed that this was the practice in many middle-class families, and she just put forward the notion casually to see what the children would think of it. She was totally unprepared for the shocked and tearful reactions that the proposition provoked in Shade and Femi.

'Don't you want to be our mother, now you have left Daddy?'

'How could you even think of such a thing? Don't you love us?'

They were both outraged and heartbroken by the very thought of changing how they addressed her.

Anna reassured them that of course she loved them. She had just thought they might like the idea of their being more equal. She abandoned the idea without further discussion, but this issue reflected a much deeper sense of insecurity in both Shade and Femi. She would have to be careful to ensure that she provided them with the security they still needed, and she must set aside her own doubts and fears in order to bolster them. They were, after all, still young, and such a major change in their lives, even though they had wanted it for a long time, would continue to present confusion and resentment until they had all adjusted to their changed situation.

CHAPTER TWENTY-FOUR

When they returned to the Wirral, they went straight to their new home in Ellesmere Port, after collecting their faithful little car and, the birds, chirping and squawking in their cages, from Anna's colleague's house. They still had very few of their own possessions, so their new house felt far from homely. It was damp, sparsely and drably furnished, with worn and ugly carpets, and situated as it was on a rather dreary estate, it felt inordinately depressing. The house itself was semi-detached, with three poky bedrooms, a lounge which also contained the stairs, and an old fashioned cramped kitchen with only the barest amenities. It was built in red brick and looked out, with its sightless eyes, on a small rather unkempt looking garden. The neighbours had been seen spying on the new arrivals from behind their net curtains. No one called to welcome them, and it was soon clear that they were in fact most unwelcome.

They had hardly been in the house more than twenty-four hours, when they received a complaint from the couple next door. Apparently their neighbours, in the house adjoining their own semi-detached, had been disturbed by the sound of hammering coming from the other side of the wall. Anna apologised, and explained that they had only been fixing the curtains, but the hostile looks she received confirmed her suspicion, that it was not so much the noise that was upsetting them, as the fact that her children were black. She realised then that this had to be a very temporary roof until she could sort out her life; there was no way they could remain in such a dismal and inhospitable place for more than six months.

'I hate it here,' said Shade, echoing all their thoughts.

Term had started, so Anna had no choice but to return to work. Ironically, although work felt like the last thing she needed, being among colleagues, people her own age, several of whom had been through divorces themselves, actually saved her sanity. Teaching also took her mind off her own problems and gave her little time to brood, at least during the day. It was worse for Shade and Femi, left behind in the house on the miserable estate. However, Femi's mind was occupied with his preparations for going off to Cambridge, so he was not too badly affected. Shade, on the other hand, felt very isolated, and this was to become worse when Femi left home at the beginning of October.

Anna continued to communicate with her lawyer on a frequent basis. Her first concern was to retrieve their personal possessions from their old home. Shola had been adamant that he had no intention of leaving the house. He maintained that Anna had left the marital home of her own accord, and that she could return any time she wanted to. Anna decided that it was not worth contesting the house situation, but did insist that they should be allowed access to collect their things. Letters passed between their respective lawyers, the latter, as always in divorce cases, becoming the main financial beneficiaries of their domestic collapse.

Eventually, a date was set by the two sets of lawyers, for them to collect their clothes, books and other possessions. Three of Anna's colleagues had agreed to help her, so a van was hired, and on the appointed day and time they and Anna arrived at the family house. Everyone had agreed that the children should not have to go through the trauma of seeing their father, so they stayed in Ellesmere Port to await the arrival of their things.

As the van drew up at the house, Anna was filled with dread, as she wondered what the state of both Shola and the house would be. She waited in the van until her colleagues had spoken to Shola at the front door.

'Come in, Anna. It's ok. We are with you, so don't worry,' one of her male colleagues reassured her.

With shaking legs, Anna climbed the steps up to her old front door. The hall was filled with black bin bags containing hers and the children's clothes; and cardboard boxes, containing their books, videos and records were stacked high against the walls. The place looked like a storage depot, with all their possessions, including some small items of furniture, scattered around at random. Anna could hear Shola's voice at an unnaturally high pitch, laughing and shouting with a Nigerian friend he had brought over from Liverpool, presumably for moral support. He was also affable, and slightly flirtatious with her female colleague, actually her line manager, who had accompanied her.

Anna slunk past the open sitting room door where he was, and headed for the basement to collect a few pots and pans, some crockery and cutlery, and other sorely needed kitchen equipment. The kitchen was tidy but had a strange stale smell, as if it had been deserted for a long time. In fact, the whole house smelt this way, as if in her leaving, the heart of the home had been cut out. Only the corpse remained and it was quietly decomposing.

Taking Chances

Anna mindlessly gathered a few items, but she could not focus on the task in hand. This had been her home, a home she had taken a pride in. Now it seemed an empty shell, the detritus of the long years of her married life. She could not wait to get out into the fresh air; she felt she could not breathe in this polluted atmosphere. She forced her mind back to her task, took only the minimum of essentials, and thankfully climbed the stairs from the basement and made for the front door.

While she had been in the kitchen, her colleagues had almost finished clearing the bags and boxes from the hall. There were also a few small items of furniture, such as a desk and a couple of bookcases, that she had personally purchased, which also had to go in the van, but the capable hands of her friends ensured that everything was under control, and the task was nearly completed. Anna could not stay in the house any longer, listening to Shola's manic laughter through the open door of the front room.

She caught the eye of one of her helpers. 'If you don't mind I think I'll wait in the van. I'm feeling a bit faint.'

'Don't worry,' he assured her. 'We've nearly finished. You go back to the van and relax.'

Gratefully, Anna crept out of the door, and out of the gate of her old home, which swung to behind her. She had no feelings left; she just wanted this trip to be over. As she sat in the van, waiting for her colleagues to complete their loading, one of them deposited a pile of old photo albums in her lap. Anna glanced at them, and as she did so, she noticed that two of the albums contained photos taken at the respective funerals of Shola's father and mother.

'These two are not mine,' she called to the colleague who had given them to her, and he duly took them from her and returned to the house. Her brief glimpse of those photos reminded her cruelly of some of the crises she and Shola had endured together. She felt sincerely full of regret, and sorry for her husband. He was totally alone in the world now. Why, oh why, had it come to this?

She had no more time to agonise. Her colleagues joined her in the van, as everything had now been loaded. They were soon on the road back to Ellesmere Port, leaving Anna's old life behind.

The next couple of weeks were busy with work, and getting Femi's things ready for his departure for Cambridge. Soon the day arrived for him to leave. He hugged Anna and Shade, and reassured them that he and they would be fine. Both kept a brave face for him, but the house would feel very empty and hollow without him. Now it was just the two women, trying to survive in a very harsh and hostile world. They felt like two survivors of a shipwreck, clinging to some flimsy driftwood, tossed about in the open sea, praying for help, but not confident that they would be rescued.

Some nights Anna would wake up in the small hours, and she would find herself trembling, her whole body shaking, terrified of what her life would become. Who was she? The only self she knew, independent of Shola, was that of a very young woman, barely a child. She had married when she was only twenty-three; she now felt as if she was twenty-three again, but with the body of a middle-aged woman. She was as insecure now as she had been then, but without the optimism and hope of youth. She would toss and turn for hours, and arrive at work the next day with a headache and an ashen face.

On other occasions she would find herself in the local supermarket, pushing her shopping trolley, and wondering what on earth she was doing there. She would look around at the other shoppers, mostly in couples, and feel terrified of the world at large. Who were all these strange people? How would she ever relate to anyone at all? She had spent virtually her whole adult life as part of a couple; now she was single again, with the feeling that she had neither the skills nor the desire to interact with the human race. All these individuals appeared to her tortured

Taking Chances

imagination as unknowable and even menacing. They were happily going about their business, while Anna's whole world had fallen apart. She was not sure whether she was an alien, looking in awe and wonderment on human kind, or whether they were the aliens, and she a frightened human being observing their antics from afar.

❦

Anna had kept in touch with Dorothy by telephone as she now had little time to go over to Liverpool because of the demands of the job. She also tried to spend as much time as she could with Shade when she was not working, and she had to pretend that she was feeling fine, so as not to alarm her daughter, or make her fear that she was having second thoughts about leaving Shola. This was far from the truth, but Anna did not know how to share her complex feelings of loss with her daughter, and did not actually understand them herself.

Accordingly, they would drive to Ellesmere Port market, and look around the fascinating array of goods on sale; sometimes they would brave a day out in Chester, with its confusing one way traffic systems, and look in its attractive little shops, or stroll around the ancient Roman walls, ending up in a quaint alleyway tea shop; at other times they would drive to one of the several beaches on the Wirral, a particular favourite being at a place named Thursaston, where there was windswept grassy country park, which bordered the wide river estuary.

One day when she was at work, after a particularly sleepless night, she found a quiet moment to telephone her friend.

'Dorothy, I feel so depressed. I'm also having what I think must be panic attacks. Sometimes as I'm driving in to work, I start crying for no reason. Then when I'm in the loo at work, I find myself weeping. What is wrong with me?'

'Anna, don't worry. It will pass. I was exactly the same when I first got back from Nigeria after leaving Jide. It just takes time to adjust, but look at me now. I have never been so happy. You will meet someone else eventually. You're only forty-nine, and you have many years to look forward to.'

'That's what's scaring me. What on earth am I going to do with my life?'

'Trust me. You will be ok. I know it.'

'Thanks, Dorothy. You always know the right thing to say.'

※

Slowly, the legal machine ground its way through the paperwork required for Anna and Shola's divorce. It had been agreed that they would have what the lawyers called a 'clean break' settlement. Anna did not request any maintenance for herself or Femi, and Shola agreed to buy her out of the house. This would mean, she hoped fervently, that she would eventually get a lump sum which would enable her to put down a deposit on a small house for her and the children.

One morning, her 'decree nisi' arrived, in an official brown envelope. Fortunately, she had not been required to attend court in person, but it was a strange sensation, reading about the death of her marriage in the cold legal language of the document. But she was now technically free, at least in law, yet no amount of legal documents would ever set her free from the bad memories and the regret that were left with her. These were things she would have to come to terms with over the following months and years.

Now at least, she could move on physically, and they could get away from the miserable house they were currently living in. Unfortunately, there would be little money left for her after her lawyers had taken their chunk of the settlement. In fact, she was shocked to find that they had siphoned off nearly half of the meagre amount she had received. She knew then that she would have to take a larger mortgage than she had anticipated, but there would be just enough money for her to put down a small deposit on a property.

Taking Chances

Anna and Shade started house hunting as soon as the settlement came through, as Shade could not wait to leave their wretched rented house. She had been forced to spend so many days alone there, applying for jobs and writing articles based on her academic studies, yet all the time conscious of the hostility around her. But she was developing a fluent journalistic style, and she had high hopes for her future in writing and research.

They soon came to realise that their available funds would not be enough for their ideal home, but they compromised. They found another ex-council house, but on a much more attractive estate in the small village of Bromborough, quite close to Anna's college. The house itself was in good condition, with three above average sized bedrooms, and was situated on a leafy avenue, within easy reach of the shops and the station. The house looked very attractive from the road, having a dormer style roof, and fresh white paintwork on the windows, gate and front door, while inside all the paintwork was new, and the wallpaper was soothing in pale green and white. Anna put in an offer on the house, and it was accepted.

Moving day came round a couple of months later, and Femi came home to help. After a hectic few hours, helping to load and unload the removal van, the three collapsed on makeshift beds in a chaotic scene of boxes, furniture placed helter skelter and other items scattered at random in every room. However, in a few days, when they had organised and stowed away their possessions, they felt a sense of euphoria. They had a place of their own, one they would not be forced to flee, and where they could be free to be themselves. Anna, especially, experienced her first feeling of satisfaction and relief since she had left her home six months previously.

She spent the next few weeks arranging her new house as its proud owner. The birds sang in their cages, which she had placed on the large window sill in her kitchen. Their plumage added some touches of colour, as they chirped and preened themselves, looking out at the pocket handkerchief sized garden at the back of the house. She purchased a plush, dark green, four piece suite of furniture, including a comfortable reclining armchair, and large footstool, for the sitting room, at an exorbitant cost, on hire purchase; but it was worth every penny in terms of her sense of accomplishment. She hung pictures on every wall in the house, placed her ornaments and plants on all available surfaces, and ensured that all the possessions they had brought with them were stowed away in their appropriate places.

She went to second hand furniture stores, and purchased additional necessary furniture and household items, and even bought a brand new cooker and washing machine, to be paid for monthly. She almost replicated the kitchen of her old home in her new one, and this brought with it an incredulous sense of achievement and pride. At least, she had been able to provide a roof for herself and the children, and she felt, for the first time in her life, in control of her own destiny.

CHAPTER TWENTY-FIVE

Six months later

The last few months had flown by. Anna, now turned fifty years old, was fully occupied with her job, and she had also decided to take a course in teaching English as a foreign language at Liverpool University. The latter required her to attend an evening class twice a week, as well as complete written assignments and prepare lessons on a regular basis. She had very little time to brood or worry, but felt subconsciously that she was preparing for the rest of her life, as Dorothy had advised.

Shade, now grown into a confident and attractive young woman, hiding the scars of her traumatic childhood very effectively, was still making applications for jobs, but she had recently decided that she wanted to focus on London, rather than stay in racist Merseyside. Anna encouraged her in this plan, which she thought made perfect sense. She herself was now wondering whether she, like Shade, should think about moving away from the area, which contained so many bad associations for her, but she was unwilling yet to contemplate selling her little house that she had fixed up so lovingly.

Anna's colleagues at work had remarked recently that she looked so much better in herself. She had not been aware of her haggard appearance over the past few years, but she did now feel ten years younger. Perhaps she even looked it. It was strange that turning fifty had not affected her in anything like the way turning forty had done, when she had felt depressed for weeks. In fact, her fiftieth birthday had energised her to look forward rather than back.

She and Shade now visited Lola and Maria at weekends. They all used to pile into the small car, and Anna would drive to the Wirral seaside towns of West Kirby or New Brighton. Maria was by now an active and vocal toddler who loved to run on the smooth sand, build sandcastles, or play in the amusement arcades. On the way back from these trips, she would demand a visit to McDonalds, able to spot the big red 'M' before she could even talk properly, and would enjoy smearing her face with brightly coloured sauces, as she tucked into her burger.

One afternoon, Anna and Shade decided to visit Millie. They had not seen her and Tom for several years, though they had kept in touch with a regular Christmas card and the occasional phone call. It felt very strange to be visiting in their old locality; so much had happened since they lived there. It was almost like being on a movie set, featuring a familiar backdrop, populated by strange people and with an unfamiliar script.

Millie and Tom were at least familiar, and they appeared totally unchanged since Anna had last seen them several years previously. Millie still wore one of her preposterously huge caftans, and Tom still smiled sheepishly, with goodwill exuding from his cheerful face, with its habitual dark five o'clock shadow.

Millie thoroughly enjoyed Anna and Shade's account of their flight from their former home, now over a year ago. In her usual jolly way, she listened large-eyed to the story and contributed humorous comments at various points. Now even Anna and Shade could see the funny side of their exploits and adventures, and they all laughed until tears rolled down their cheeks as their story unfolded. They shared one of Millie's delicious home baked cakes and a pot of tea, and her infectious good humour.

The visit cheered both Anna and Shade immeasurably, and they felt almost light hearted as they bade goodbye to this simple and kindly couple.

Millie's parting shot to Shade had them laughing all the way to the car.

'Watch your mother doesn't run off with a Chinaman!' she quipped once again as she had so many times before.

'You won't, will you, Mummy?' asked Shade mock seriously as they drove away.

※

A few days later, Anna was in her staffroom at the college. The autumn term was well under way as it was mid-October. She was busy marking some student essays, and when the shared telephone rang one of her colleagues picked it up.

'Anna, it's for you,' said Joe, one of the Maths lecturers, as he held out the receiver to her.

Anna took the receiver and held it to her ear. The voice at the other end was a man's, and was unfamiliar.

'Yes, this is Mrs Banjo speaking,' she confirmed.

'Mrs Banjo, I have your husband here. He's in a very bad way. Will you speak to him?'

Anna's stomach turned over, and she felt sick. She had had no contact with Shola, except through their lawyers, for more than a year. His distinctive figure had been sighted by various people in Birkenhead, and even once by Anna, in Hamilton Square, as she sped through the town in her car. But she had not spoken directly to him since she gone to the house with the police on that fateful night the previous year.

'I don't feel I can speak to him,' she stammered.

'Please do. I am a priest and your husband has come to me as he is desperate to talk to you, and has asked me to intercede on his behalf.'

'But you don't know any of the circumstances, at least not from my perspective. How can you ask this of me?'

'I'm just asking you to show some pity for this poor man.'

Anna's instinct was to slam down the telephone receiver, but very reluctantly she agreed to the priest's request, feeling that she had no choice but to speak to Shola.

Shola started by saying how devastated he had been without Anna. He said that he missed her. He claimed that he did not understand how the divorce could have gone through with so much speed, and that he was sorry for all the harm he had done her.

'But you never showed me any love, at least not in recent years,' she replied. 'We could not even speak to each other, and you have traumatised the children. I'm not sure whether they will ever recover from the kind of childhood you inflicted on them.'

'This is because of my culture. You don't understand.'

'This is not any excuse, Shola. I have known many Nigerians who are kind and loving to their children and who know how to express their emotions.'

'But my childhood was hard. My mother abandoned me to my father's care for two years when I was very small, while she went away to Ghana as a trader. I never learned how to be a loving parent. Anyway, it's not all my fault. You caused problems too. You were too soft with the children and then blamed me for disciplining them.'

'Stop there, Shola. I didn't want to have this conversation, but I am glad you have just said what you did. It has confirmed for me that my decision to leave was the right one. You have made it clear that you haven't actually thought about why I had to leave you, or made any effort to change the way you think. Now I have nothing else to say to you. There's absolutely no point.'

'Please, Anna. Please give me another chance. I can't go on without you.'

'It's too late for that. I have moved on. You should too.'

'You have changed. You have become hard.'

'I've had to. You must get on with your life. I do wish you all the best, but our relationship is over. I must go now.'

With trembling hands, Anna replaced the receiver firmly and walked back to her desk. Her mind was whirling and she felt as if she was about to vomit.

One of her colleagues placed a fresh mug of coffee on her desk. Anna cupped her hands around its warmth, and tried to calm her racing thoughts. She knew she had done the right thing. How can you live with a person whom you wished dead? How could that be good for that person, even if he did not know what you were thinking? Surely the negative vibes would poison their object and everything surrounding him.

She wished that Shola would find a new partner, but she was not very positive about the success of this. Who would put up with the kind of life he had subjected her to all those years? Well, perhaps he would change, but deep down she doubted it. Anyway, it was no longer her problem. She was moving on, even if he wanted to pull her back and down again; she was no longer in his power.

Anna felt shaken up for a few days after her conversation with Shola. She did not mention anything about it to Shade, as she knew that it would frighten her. She would be afraid that Anna might weaken and return to him. Anna knew within herself that she had moved far beyond this now, and that she would never return to her odious existence of the past. But Shade had seen her weaken too many times in the past, and even now might not fully believe that her mother had changed.

❦

One evening, a few days after her traumatic conversation with Shola, Anna was browsing through the local paper. Her eye was caught by an advertisement, publicising a forthcoming event at a nearby hotel. A clairvoyant, Rosa, was offering consultations to the public. The fee looked reasonable, and Anna was drawn to the idea of looking into what her future might hold. She vaguely remembered her mother always maintaining, that a fortune teller had correctly predicted the first name initial of her husband to be, long before she had even met him. Anna had been sceptical then, but now she was in dire need of something, anything, that might reassure her, or inspire her with faith in her future.

On the specified evening, Anna set off to consult Rosa. She told Shade that she was going to visit a friend, as she was unwilling to have cold water thrown over her hopes and expectations; she also did not want to be seen as gullible or naive, in the eyes of her now grown up daughter.

Anna arrived at the hotel named in the paper. It was a country hotel in what looked like a converted eighteenth century manor house, and was situated up a sweeping drive, in attractive grounds. The garden in front of the house was devoted to lawns and flowering shrubs, with a huge cedar tree spreading its branches on a lower lawn at the back of the building. In the distance, she could see a vast golf course, punctuated with old oak and sycamore trees, as well as gorse, clumps of hazel, and other varieties of small trees and bushes.

The car park was almost full, but Anna managed to inch her red Micra into a small available space, between the larger and more expensive cars. She entered the lobby of the hotel rather nervously, as she had no idea of what to expect. She noticed a large poster advertising Rosa's talents and services, together with a rather indistinct photograph of the clairvoyant, on a board just inside the front door, which also directed prospective clients into a lounge, opening off to the right of the lobby.

Anna followed the sign, and found herself in a wood panelled room, furnished elegantly, and providing comfortable seating for a large number of people. There was a bar at one end of the room which offered coffee and tea, as well as alcoholic drinks. What struck Anna immediately, was that all the occupants of the plush sofas and chairs were female, the majority about her own age.

Anna bought herself a coffee, and registered her details, at the same time paying for a session with Rosa. She was asked to take a seat and wait for her name to be called. Fortunately Anna was able to locate an empty armchair where she sat down, placing her cup on an occasional table beside the chair. Then she furtively looked around at her fellow clients.

The woman sitting next to her was thin and gaunt, with dyed blonde hair and heavy make up. She was in her late forties or early fifties, from what Anna was able to judge. She was dressed in rather old, but still elegant clothes, which had obviously once been very expensive. She was smoking a cigarette in between sips of coffee, and her expression was tense and anxious.

'Have you seen Rosa, before?' Anna asked her timidly.

'Yes, a few times. She's very good,' replied the woman.

She seemed unwilling to say any more, so Anna occupied herself by observing the other women in the room. Some looked anxious, like her neighbour, while others were happily smiling and chatting to whoever was sitting near them. What they all shared, it seemed to Anna, was a fever to know what life had in store for them, and they trusted Rosa to give them the hope or consolation that they needed. They were all waiting, like characters in 'Waiting for Godot', for vital solutions to the problems of their lives.

One by one the women were called in for their appointments. On leaving, they appeared to almost float, or sleep walk, to the door, looking neither to the right nor left, seemingly oblivious to the others waiting, being entirely preoccupied with whatever Rosa had told them.

Soon Anna heard her name being called. She followed the directions to the room where Rosa was doing her consultations.

Rosa looked entirely normal: Anna had been expecting an eccentric, larger than life character, like the stock fortune tellers she had read about in novels, or seen in films on television. Rosa was plump, was probably in her forties, and had her auburn hair done up in a large bun; she possessed keen, but kindly blue eyes and greeted Anna with a warm smile.

'Do sit down,' she invited. 'Have you ever had a reading before?'

'No,' replied Anna. 'This is my first time.'

'Would you like a palm reading, cards or crystal ball?'

'I don't know,' said Anna, feeling stupid. 'What do you advise for me?'

'Well, for your first time, perhaps we will just do a palm reading and I will also look into the crystal ball. Is this alright with you?'

'Fine,' replied Anna, feeling totally out of her depth, and even a bit scared.

Rosa read Anna's palm and made a few general comments, such as that Anna had a long life line, broken by a major event from which she would recover, and then she consulted her crystal ball.

As she looked at the ball, she observed that Anna had been through a difficult time, but that she had the strength to survive and remake her life.

'Will I ever be happy again?' asked Anna, her voice shaking a little.

'Yes, you will', replied Rosa confidently. 'You are a basically strong person, with the will to survive and prosper. You will never be rich, but you will have enough to live comfortably. You will be around for a long time, and you will not die of anything nasty.'

'That's a relief,' Anna observed. 'But will I ever have another relationship?'

'Definitely,' said Rosa. 'Just don't give up on life. Go out, meet new people and you will find love. You have a lot to give and there will be someone out there for you.'

Anna thanked Rosa profusely at the end of her session. She, like the other women, walked out of the building on Cloud Nine, feeling so much better about her life. Rosa was a good psychologist, if nothing else, but Anna could not help feeling that she did indeed have special powers, and was able to use these powers to help her fellow human beings, particularly women, in their hour of need. Faith was all that was required, and Anna was receptive and ready to have that faith. God had not given up on her; life could be good again.

※

One afternoon the following week, Anna finished her classes early. Normally, she would have gone straight home. Today instead she drove her car into Eastham, the village where her college was situated, and found her way to a promontory overlooking the river. She parked her car and got out. The leaves had changed colour and were falling one by one, carpeting the ground in their rich yellows and browns. The afternoon was mild, and the sun was shining from a sky containing small fleecy white clouds, drifting slowly across the blue expanse above her. There were a few walkers exercising their dogs on the tracks beside the river, but all was very quiet and serene.

Anna strolled along the river bank until she found a seat in the sun overlooking the muddy shore, with a view of the distant water. She sat down and let her thoughts drift gently. She reviewed her life, her mistakes, but no longer with such a strong sense of regret as she had used to do. There was no point in dwelling on the negative, as she could not go back and live her life again. If she was to be happy, she must learn from the past but not be a victim of it. So, she had been immature, a mere child, when she married. She had been unable to face the consequences of her early mistake, and had tried to ignore the descent of her marriage into a morass of resentment and recrimination. In her desire not to become yet another statistic, she had jeopardised the happiness and even the lives of her children. But that was the past; the future was still there to be lived fruitfully. She had got out just in time.

Anna could not but pity Shola and regret the broken man he had become, and she blamed herself for her share in bringing him to this condition. She prayed that he might emerge from the past, as she was trying to do, into a better understanding of himself, which he could use to make a healthier and more positive life in the future. Perhaps, like a snake shedding its old skin, he would emerge renewed and re-invigorated. Maybe he would decide to return to Nigeria, and re-engage with the career he had left behind there, and free from the crushing pressure of racism, achieve his potential in the academic world. But that was for him to do: it was no longer either her responsibility or even her concern.

Unlike Shola, she still had her children, her lovely handsome and clever children. They were the positive outcome of her marriage, and they would not have existed if it were not for her union with Shola. Yes, they would face difficulties in life, but she believed they were fine enough to rise above them. She knew that they had all emerged traumatised by their childhood, and that they would each have to come to terms with this, as well as their racial identity, in their own different ways. She vowed to be a better mother to them all now, and she would try to make up to them her failings of the past.

For herself, she still had years stretching before her, and she now had the freedom to be herself, and the maturity to avoid repeating her past mistakes. Why be afraid? She would start again: maybe she would meet someone else with whom to share the second half of her life. She had at least learned some

Taking Chances

important lessons, and gained a measure of wisdom, in the half century she had already lived.

Anna remembered Dorothy's words the night she had fled her marital home.

'You have your chance. Now take it.'

She had taken that offered chance. And now she would take more chances, all the chances she was offered or she would make for herself. Her life was not over; it was just beginning.

The afternoon was slipping away. The sky was clouding over and the breeze was becoming chilly.

I must get home for tea. Shade will be expecting me, Anna reminded herself.

She got up and slowly strolled back to her waiting car. She climbed into the car, and sat motionless inside for a few seconds. Then she switched on the engine and backed carefully out of her parking space. Anna turned her car in the direction of home. As she did so, the sun emerged from the clouds for its last burst of light and warmth in the shortening day.

About the Author

Frances Xanthos Christodoulou was born in 1946 to a Greek father and English mother. She has lived in the United States and Nigeria as well as Britain, frequently visits Cyprus and Greece, and is the mother of three now adult children.

Educated at Manchester University, and at the University of Massachusetts in Amherst, F.X. Christodoulou has been a teacher/lecturer in English Language and Literature for most of her working life. Now retired she is realising a long held ambition to write fiction, though she has previously published an academic textbook on study skills.

Her personal experiences and observations, as well as her imagination, have inspired her writing, as has her desire to share her insights and ideas with her readers. She is currently working on her second novel.

F.X. Christodoulou lives in London with her Greek Cypriot husband.

Printed in the United Kingdom
by Lightning Source UK Ltd.
132239UK00001B/31-48/P